GO INTO THE CITY

And the Lord said unto him, Arise, and go into the city, and it shall be told thee what thou must do.

Acts 9:6

GO INTO THE CITY

Sermons for a Strenuous Age

JOHN COMPTON LEFFLER

Foreword by John E. Hines

MADRONA PUBLISHERS
SEATTLE • 1986

Copyright © 1986 by the Rector, Wardens, and Vestrymen of Saint Mark's Parish
All rights reserved
Printed in the United States of America

Published by Madrona Publishers, Inc.
P.O. Box 22667
Seattle, Washington 98122

10   9   8   7   6   5   4   3   2   1

Library of Congress Cataloging-in-Publication Data

Leffler, John Compton, 1900-
   Go into the city.

   1. Christian life — 1960-   —Addresses, essays, lectures. I. Title.
BV4501.2.L428 1986   248.4   85-23366
ISBN 0-88089-014-2

TO MY WIFE, FAITH GILLIES LEFFLER,
AND FOR OUR SONS, BROOKS GILLIES,
JOHN ANDREW, AND TIMOTHY COMPTON.

Foreword

BY JOHN E. HINES

JOHN Compton Leffler—a man to be reckoned with in the Episcopal Church in the twentieth century. Born in the state of New York into the great Wesleyan tradition in the Methodist Church precisely at the turn of the century, he is an example of the powerful shaping influence of hereditary genes. His great-grandfather was the first pioneer circuit rider, for Methodism, in the Ohio Valley. His father was an ordained pastor in the Methodist Church. How could John Compton Leffler escape the pull of such compelling antecedents? How could he possibly escape the ministry of preaching the word? John Leffler escaped neither.

He was ordained into the Methodist ministry in 1922 and served that church until 1927. Fortunately for the Episcopal Church, always in need of effective preachers of the Gospel, Leffler came within the orbit of one of the Episcopal Church's most illustrious bishops and dedicated ecumenists, Charles Henry Brent, Bishop of Western New York. It was at Bishop Brent's hands that John Leffler received the grace of orders in the Episcopal Church. Here again, the gifts of an intense missionary zeal and an unflagging concern for the "coming great Church," so central to Brent's vision, appear to have been transmitted by the laying on of hands. John Leffler never lost the imprimatur of that world-vision of mission. His preaching consistently reflects a single-minded dedication to both of these concerns.

Wherever John Leffler served the Lord Jesus Christ through the Episcopal Church, preaching appears to be a major, though not the only, persuasive element in the arsenal of his varied and thorough ministry. He began at St. Paul's, Rochester, New York, already known for its strong pulpit. He created "a great cloud of witnesses" with his timely, always biblically-oriented sermons from the pulpit of St. John's, Ross, California, and later from St. Luke's, San Francisco—the latter parish virtually under the eaves of Grace Cathedral. The beautiful, exotic, cosmopolitan city of San Francisco, with its broad cultural and ethnic diversity, proved to be an ideal setting for John Leffler's perceptive preaching and compassionate pastoral ministry. He is still gratefully remembered for his strong protest of the U.S. government's interning of American-born Japanese families following the bombing of Pearl Harbor. It was no small challenge, ministry on the West Coast in those years. Definitely no place for an amateur or a sentimentalist. John Leffler proved equal to the task. When one notes, in the far-too-modest listing of honors and responsibilities that accrued to him during his ministry, a line that says: "Instructor in Homiletics, Church Divinity School of the Pacific, 1937–1940," one must conclude that dozens of embryo preachers were both stretched and rewarded by virtue of sitting at the feet of so talented a teacher.

It seemed only natural and appropriate that such an able administrator and effective practitioner of the art of preaching should next appear as Dean of St. Mark's Cathedral in Seattle, that fortresslike church reminiscent of Durham, England, astride the highest ridge of the Northwest's most enterprising city. For the next two decades, 1951 to 1971, Dean Leffler pursued not just a citywide ministry but one which evoked regional and national acclaim. Half of that ministry was in harness with one of the Episcopal Church's brightest episcopal stars—the late Stephen F. Bayne, Bishop of Olympia, a cogent and persuasive interpreter of the Christian verities. It would be difficult to discover in the Episcopal Church of the twentieth century a bishop-dean combination capable of matching the one in Seattle during those creative years. No one was surprised when the Episcopal Church's House of Deputies, one of this nation's largest deliberative bodies, underlined its respect and affection for Dean Leffler by elevating him to the vice-presidency, a crowning honor marking a distinguished vocation and career in the Church.

Foreword

This collection of sermons by Dean Leffler represents his accumulation of faith, wisdom, humor, candor, healthy skepticism, acute perception, all distilled from fifty years of ministry in the real world and in the name of Christ Jesus. Many who read the sermons will count it deprivation not to have heard them preached. For effective preaching, as Phillips Brooks—one of Dean Leffler's role models—defined it, is "truth mediated through personality."

Preface

SOMEONE eighty-five years old and partially blind does not often publish a book. It is my friends who have urged me to do it and have made it possible.

Life is like a jig-saw puzzle, and the older one gets the more one finds that the pieces fit. A basic piece in the making of my own life was my Methodist background. My father, John Ford Leffler, was not a typical Methodist preacher; he was not a powerful speaker and he did not like the revival meetings he had to join in the small towns of western New York and north-central Pennsylvania. He loved the theatre and used to sneak off to Buffalo and spend his time watching a play or a vaudeville show. He probably would have made a good Episcopalian. By the time he entered the ministry at the age of thirty he had been a wood turner and a railroad section boss, with a first-hand knowledge of the world's sins and virtues. His congregations loved him and never wanted him to leave; he was a pastor such as very few I've known.

Preface

I was born May 26, 1900, in the country parsonage of the North Ridge Methodist Church, north of Niagara Falls. I was a healthy ten-pound infant but had two badly clubbed feet. My father almost lost his faith in God and came close to leaving the ministry, but Mother said, "Thank God it's his feet, not his head. We'll find a way to fix them." And find it she did. But it took ten operations and casts and braces on my legs until I was six years old.

Nevertheless, it was a happy growing up. My parents handled my disability with great skill, never becoming oversolicitous. For this I shall always be grateful, because all my life I've had to deal with pain and the consequences of that early infirmity, and I have been able to do so with some degree of success.

There were advantages to being a cripple. To be sure, I could not join in the strenuous play of my younger brother Paul and other children, but I did learn how to be happy alone. I became fascinated with letters and words and, with Mother to instruct me, began to read at three. I had an imaginary playmate named Jesus to whom I could talk about childish concerns. He did not answer me but he always listened and always was there.

My mother, Lena Compton Leffler, was the greatest influence in the early years of my life because I had to spend a great deal of time at home. I can remember her doing the dishes or scrubbing clothes on the washboard, singing gospel hymns in her wonderful voice as she worked. She was from Congregational stock on her mother's side, descended from one Thomas Brigham who arrived in New England in 1640, and of Methodist stock on her father's—the Comptons, who settled in the Hudson River country and upstate New York. The Comptons were descended from the Earl of Compton, known as one of the worst rakes in the court of William the Conqueror, so none of us can be sure of legitimacy in that line. The most colorful ancestor was not English but Dutch—a pirate who sacked Morocco and carried off three shiploads of booty, including a Moorish princess whom he installed in a residence said to be palatial. At least that was the story told to me in the parsonage.

Dad was anxious that I have the education he lacked and encouraged me to become an excellent student. He sacrificed to help send me to Wesleyan University, a good Methodist school in Middletown, Connecticut.

The United States had just entered World War I when the preacher's kid moved out of the parsonage and began to enjoy his freedom and show some rebellion. I did not distinguish myself at Wesleyan, but I did enjoy the great preachers who came to the campus every Sunday. I was still feeling rebellious when, as I was about to graduate, I decided, what the hell, I'll go to seminary and see if I like it—and I did.

I spent a year at Garrett Theological Seminary on the campus of Northwestern University in Evanston, Illinois,

Preface

spending most of my time with two outstanding Old Testament scholars who made me see the prophets as great preachers and with a New Testament scholar who opened the gospels and the letters of Paul to my mind and my heart. Then I entered the Methodist ministry and was in it for five years—not the happiest time of my life because my love of music and drama and liturgy ran straight against the customs of a little suburban Methodist church.

One night at a midnight service at St. Paul's Episcopal Church in Rochester, New York, as I was kneeling to receive the sacrament, it suddenly came over me with a warm glow—"John, this is where you belong"—and for two years I kept that idea before me until Bishop Charles Henry Brent brought me into the Episcopal Church. Coincidentally, I became an assistant for two years at St. Paul's.

By then I had been married for three years, having convinced Faith Gillies, the daughter of a prominent local minister, to let another preacher into her life. But I found myself wanting to leave Rochester; I wanted to get away from feeling I was simply the son and son-in-law of two better-known preachers. Perhaps a touch of rebellion remained.

I accepted a call from Bishop Edward Lambe Parsons, my "patron saint," the Bishop of California, and I took the rectorate of St. John's in Ross, a small, plush parish just north of San Francisco. The Depression arrived one month later. Those were eleven difficult years. Nevertheless, what had been a family chapel became a church that reached out to the entire community and is still one of the strongest parishes in the Diocese of California.

From there I accepted the call to become a preaching rector at St. Luke's on Van Ness Avenue in San Francisco, known to local clergy as "the beautiful mausoleum on automobile row." On my first Sunday, there was a male choir, an excellent organist, a beautiful church—and fifty people in the congregation.

After another eleven years, Bishop Stephen F. Bayne came to see me. My heart sank because I knew it had to do with St. Mark's Cathedral in Seattle. I'd heard the story: closure for bankruptcy and lots of problems. Grimy, dirty, with a wheezing organ and small congregation. My predecessor, Richard Watson, and Bishop S. Arthur Huston had reopened the parish, but there was still much to be done. Eventually, of course, I accepted the rectorate. As it worked out, at St. Mark's I was able to use all of my abilities: organizing, pastoral counseling, and, particularly, preaching. It was there, twenty years later, that my ministry concluded on December 31, 1971. Among the highlights of those twenty years were the construction of Cathedral House and Bloedel Auditorium and the installation of the magnificent organ built by Flentrop of Holland, one of the finest organs in the world.

Forty-nine of my years were shared with my wife, Faith. I met her in the autumn of 1922 when I was assistant at Asbury

Preface

Methodist Church in Rochester and I called on her parents, Andrew and Martha Gillies. They were also the parents of Brooks Gillies, a good friend of mine from Wesleyan who had been lost in 1920 while sailing on Lake Ontario when a violent storm came up. Dr. Gillies, a noted preacher, was recovering from a serious emotional collapse.

He told me that day that shortly after Brooks' death he had sensed the presence of Jesus and Brooks; Brooks had said, "Dad, I am with Jesus and he has asked me to help you get well." His recovery began that day and a few years later he became the chief minister at the Third Presbyterian Church in Rochester, holding large congregations spellbound with his thoughts and words. Dr. Gillies introduced me to the public sermons of Phillips Brooks, the late nineteenth-century rector of Trinity Church in Boston, the finest preacher of modern times. His son had been named for Brooks, and Faith and I gave the name to our first son, Brooks Gillies Leffler.

Faith and I were married by our fathers on January 28, 1924, at her parents' home. It had been very difficult to persuade her to marry me. Having grown up under the eyes of her father's congregations, she had sworn she would never marry a minister.

Our married life began in the parsonage of the Methodist Church in Fairport, a suburb of Rochester. It was a poorly built house with inadequate heat, furnished with cast-offs from parishioners' homes. My salary was $1,800. Faith drove the Model T into Rochester to teach English and math at East High School and sold insurance after school. Fairport was small and I got around on foot.

Faith treated any house we lived in as if it were her own. She loved to garden and spent much of her spare time growing flowers, planting shrubbery, and making a bare yard beautiful. Particularly at St. Mark's, she was a driving force of the garden guild. Open any large book in my library and you will find, pressed between the pages, flowers and leaves picked on her walks.

She never held an office in the parish and never tried to run me or the church. Faith, who might have been a career woman, as many clergy wives are today, felt that her task was to be a support to my ministry.

She had a genius for hospitality to those in need. During the Depression, she housed two couples in an apartment over our garage for two years. During World War II, when service families with children faced signs that said "No children" wherever they looked for housing, she said, "Damn the zoning code!" and turned our large third floor into an apartment for Army, Navy, Marine, and Medical Corps families. She met travel-worn brides-to-be and took them home for baths, hair-dos, and pressing of clothes before their weddings. Finally, a year before my retirement, she made a home for two Nigerian students.

My best friend, my kindest critic on preaching, a wonderful mother; a happy, intelligent, and accomplished lady, she will never read these words. Faith has been in a nursing home for over ten years, a victim of Alzheimer's disease.

The peculiar temptations of a preacher are the temptations of anyone who tries to sway the minds and emotions of people. The first, I think, is adulation. If you are any good at all, people will compliment you; you will get a reputation for being a good preacher and it can make you insufferably conceited. Second, there is the danger of being a false prophet. The Old Testament has many references to false prophets, who tell people what they want to hear and make them feel good and comfortable and safe. Since you are responsible for an organization and want to succeed, there is always the temptation to soften the blow. Another temptation is to fall back on a facility with words. Words are wonderful and I've loved them ever since I was a child, but you must be very sure that what you say is what you mean: if you do not make your meaning clear, you are in danger of being a false prophet. I guess the worst temptation of preaching is the temptation to say the right words, give the right interpretation, and not live up to it. St. Paul once said he was terrified that after preaching to others, he himself would be a castaway. Any preacher who is conscientious about God must always remember that.

Before I came to understand the Old Testament prophets, I had thought a prophet was someone who foretold the future, but I learned that if the prophets foretold the future it was because they were seeing in the future the results of what was happening in their own time.

Prophetic preaching today deals with the social issues of our age. There were times when I was preaching in the prophetic tradition, and other times when I preached to the personal needs of people. Styles of preaching have changed, but the subjects are timeless.

A preacher who can reach people has to have a touch of the actor. He's trying to do the same thing an actor would: stir the emotions, reach the minds, and keep the attention of his listeners. He has to be able to state the truth in terms people can remember, and state it simply and clearly. This is what I strove for. Keep sermons no longer than fifteen minutes, stick to one point, and have the congregation hope that you'll continue, rather than wish you would quit. A preacher has to learn not to avoid the good stopping places.

The Christian religion, as I see it, has to do with all of life, or with none. A sermon is therefore but the fallible human attempt of the preacher at one time or another to deal with the totality of the human lot as Jesus dealt with it.

Personal commitment to the God of Love, Jesus reveals, is basic for us all, whether we occupy a pulpit or listen from a pew. That commitment involves growth in our own knowledge and love of the God who loves all men, but that is tested not by public worship, loyalty to a church, or religiosity in priests. The real test comes in the busy and often hostile metropolitan centers in which the majority of us live.

Preface

"Everyone preaches only one sermon" is an old saying that I expect is true. I think that if anything could characterize the sermons which appear in this book, it would be the relevance of the living Christ to any particular time. What he said, what he did, is as true today as it was two thousand years ago. Whatever or wherever I have preached, Christ and his gospel of love are at the center. Because I feel closer to Christ than to any human being, my sermons are Christ-centered whether I am preaching from the Old or New Testament.

As I look at the world that has been so turbulent during all the years of my ministry, I wonder what is the use of preaching. The answer was given by Paul when he said he continued preaching because here and there is a person who responds and in whom a change is effected. That person becomes a new creature. If I have reached one or two people in a congregation and made some change in their lives, I figure it's been worthwhile. Because Paul was a city man who made the simple gospel preached in the countryside around Palestine pertinent to the brawling, cosmopolitan cities of the Roman Empire, I, a city man also, have leaned strongly upon him.

I've had a happy life, a long one, a tough one, and a life full of the spirit of the living Christ, who has been my companion, my friend, my chastiser, and the one whose spirit has seen me through to this time.

Acknowledgements

THE ORIGIN of this book was in the minds and hearts of two dear friends, Bernard and Jean Haldane, who suggested the project to me.

Because of my blindness, I could not have undertaken the task without the help and loyalty of my friend and editor, Janet Fitzalan Johnston, who suggested and orchestrated the process by which it was edited.

Original handwritten manuscripts were read onto tapes voluntarily by John Campbell, and especially by Tom Huntley, a professional reader to the blind.

Tape recordings were transcribed by Ruth Wolf, and in the main by Ola Gara.

Financing was begun by Rosa Claringbould and Elizabeth Jackson on behalf of my Bible class at St. Mark's Cathedral, and the gauntlet picked up by the Vestry of St. Mark's with the hearty approval of my friend and successor, Dean Cabell Tennis. My good friends Dr. Robert H. Barnes and John

Acknowledgements

Rolfe raised the necessary funds to achieve this book, and Delos McNutt served the Vestry as business manager during the publication process.

A special appreciation to my friend and publisher, Dan Levant, a secular Jew, for his understanding and sensitive insight into my Christianity.

My boundless gratitude to Dorothy Stimson Bullitt and the staff of KING-TV in Seattle for allowing me since 1953 to extend my ministry to a wider audience.

To my many generous friends, who wish to remain anonymous, who with love and faith have contributed to the support of this work, my lasting gratitude and deepest love.

To those congregations of St. John's, Ross, California; St. Luke's, San Francisco; and St. Mark's Cathedral, Seattle, who listened, criticized, and encouraged the sermons of this one preacher over the past fifty years, my eternal indebtedness.

Contents

ONE

1. The Foolishness of Preaching	3
2. Variety, the Spice of Religion	9
3. The Strenuous Life	15
4. Beyond Facts	22
5. God's Standard Wage	29
6. Paradoxes	34
7. The Sacraments	40
8. Doubt As Faith's Servant	47
9. Life Is a Quest	52
10. The Will to Believe	58

Contents

TWO

11. The Human Moses	67
12. Parables of the Kingdom	72
13. God's Decisions	77
14. God's Healing Power	83
15. Seek Ye the Lord	88
16. The Resurrection of the Dead	94
17. The Comfortable Gospel	100
18. Finding Life Right Here	106
19. Dependence on God	112
20. The Triumph of the Son of Man	118

THREE

21. Words	127
22. Patience	132
23. Contentment	138
24. With a Quiet Mind	144
25. Kindness	150
26. Is Morality Relative?	156
27. Morality Begins in the Home	163

28. Making Marriage Work	*170*
29. Love, the Basis for Moral Living	*177*
30. The Pursuit of Happiness—The Promise of Joy	*185*

FOUR

31. God in the Garden	*195*
32. Life's Ups and Downs	*201*
33. The Forgiveness of Sins	*207*
34. The Sin of Inferiority	*217*
35. Three In One— One In Three	*224*
36. Religion's Part in War and Peace	*231*
37. The Gift of the Spirit	*238*
38. The Meaning of Sainthood	*244*
39. The Uncomfortable Pulpit	*249*
40. Priesthood	*256*

ONE

Stand firm in your faith, be courageous, be strong. Let all that you do be done in love.
1 Corinthians 16:13

1

The Foolishness of Preaching

EVERY man who undertakes the awful task of preaching the gospel agrees at times with Paul that it is a foolish occupation. From the human standpoint, preaching is hard work, not only in the speaking but in the preparation. The choice of subjects is both limitless and restricted. Yet Paul believed as I do that the gospel is concerned with all of man's life on this planet, both personal and social, and if a man has a natural curiosity and interest in the rapidly unfolding human scene around him, there is no limit to what he might speak about. Yet everything a preacher says from the pulpit at a service of worship must be said within the context of the gospel of Christ. He must know and be concerned with many aspects of life: sociology, economics, psychology, politics, history, and so on, but a sermon is not a lecture on any one of these subjects nor is the pulpit a public forum. So while the subjects are limitless, the gospel itself places definite limits on the handling of them.

Preaching is also hard work in the preparation—the meaning of words, clarity of expression, the logical development of ideas, knowing what to leave out, as well as what to put in. All this results in many false starts, wasted moments, and frantic frustration when ideas do not jell and words prove elusive. For example, I happen to be one who has found using a manuscript the best means for my own preaching. This means writing what I have to say beforehand. Sometimes a sermon will flow easily from the pen, but often the script will wind up in the wastebasket, and when that happens, I wonder why on earth I ever got myself into this foolish business in the first place. This stress is intensified by the necessity of meeting a deadline on Sunday morning.

Preaching depends to no small extent on the inspiration of mind and will, but since the scriptures say the spirit like the wind "blows where it wills, . . . but you do not know whence it comes or whither it goes" (John 3:8), there is no guarantee that it will be blowing in my direction on Sunday morning, or at the time when, in desperation, I squeeze out a few hours to get my thoughts on paper. Nor is there any guarantee that I shall be adequately inspired. As I used to say to students in homiletics in church divinity school, if a man could ring the church bell and gather a congregation when the inspiration strikes, he would always be a good preacher. But alas, I doubt if my people would care to be awakened at three o'clock in the morning to hear what is burning to be said.

The Foolishness of Preaching

But enough of the human side of this foolishness, because what St. Paul really means is that God himself seems foolish to think that preaching will accomplish what he expects. That's an astounding thing to say, isn't it? To charge God with being a fool. But let's think about it for a few moments.

In the first place it seems ridiculous for God to trust men to speak for him to their fellows. Over the centuries since Amos, the illiterate shepherd, first preached in the streets of Samaria, God has spoken more often through unlikely men than through the naturally gifted. There have been only a few real giants like Paul or St. John Chrysostom, Luther, Wesley, and Phillips Brooks in the Christian tradition. Jesus had no such among the twelve disciples; Peter's first sermon on the streets of Jerusalem at Pentecost, as recorded in the Book of the Acts, is not particularly profound.

Yes, God is foolish enough to use whom he can get and to entrust the most unlikely man with the privilege of being his spokesman. God is also recklessly extravagant in using the speech of little men to get his message across. Jesus makes this quite clear in the first story he ever told, the parable of the sower and the seed (Matthew 13:18). He likens preaching to the farmer, scattering seed by hand. Much of that seed is wasted. Some lands on the shoulder of the road and the birds eat it. Other falls on the rocks and takes root quickly, but the soil is too shallow and the sun too hot, so it withers and dies. Still other seed lands amid weeds and is soon choked to death. Only part of the seed has a chance to grow in good ground and reach maturity.

Every preacher knows what this story means. Try as he will to sow good seed, he is no more effective than the ground on which it falls; in other words, the people to whom he speaks. With some, what he says is literally "for the birds." With others it takes quick root and as quickly dies. With more it is choked by the weeds of life, the anxieties, the cares, the material concerns of our existence. So the preacher often asks himself and asks God to what purpose he speaks and why all this foolish waste of time. But he does well to remember what happens when the seed of the gospel falls in a heart and mind where the soil is ready, and healthy growth brings forth thirty, sixty, or a hundred ripened seeds to compensate for the wasted ones.

When I look back over fifty years of preaching, I remember the few who, in response to my poor words, have borne much fruit, and in that recollection I no longer think God foolish nor my efforts either. Nor can man tell where the seed lands or what happens to it. More than once some total stranger has thanked me for something I said which I no longer remember but which made a lasting difference in his life. But above all else, the gospel itself is utterly foolish, as St. Paul points out. The preaching of the cross is folly to men who are perishing. It makes no sense to those for whom power consists of material wealth and physical strength. If we are honest with ourselves, the gospel of love seems like utter nonsense.

What significance does it have in the ruthless competitive struggle of our day and in every aspect of our common life? And when it comes to Christ's resurrection and living presence in the hearts of men, what could be harder to believe in our sophisticated age, and even harder to experience in our busy lives? Far harder, we may assume, than in the crowded streets of Corinth when Paul preached the folly of Christ. But he also went on to tell us that man is not saved by his own knowledge and wisdom, nor does power derive from either. God despaired of achieving his purpose that way, so he sent Jesus into the world to preach an impossible gospel which man did not want to hear and for which they nailed Jesus to the cross. Yet out of this foolish undertaking has come a wisdom and power to those who accept it such as man can find nowhere else. The foolishness of God is therefore wiser than the highest wisdom man can achieve, and the weakness of God in Christ on his cross is stronger by far than the strength of man.

When I am tempted, as every preacher is, to despair of a task which seems at times to be so foolish, I am reminded by my Christ that what has always been true is still true. Men's souls are still lost in darkness and they are afraid of the shadow of death. Men still long for some word to be spoken which has meaning for their lives. And God, for some strange and inscrutable reason, still depends upon men to speak that word as best they can by his grace. And when my Lord speaks to me thus, I go on in fear and trembling, but possessed of a joy which comes from attempting the impossible. Like all preachers I would not play the fool nor speak silly unimportant things, but I don't mind at all being a fool for Christ's sake if only the truth may occasionally shine through to other men's hearts and minds, and my own life measure up in some way to what I preach. Foolish or not, preaching is a great business.

2

Variety, the Spice of Religion

"Variety is the spice of life," runs the familiar old proverb. In fact that old saying might be called the motto of contemporary life. Our many dashings here and yon, the swing of the pendulum between work and pleasure, the swift changes of scene and activity, make the lives of most of us a ceaseless pursuit of variety. Variety is also the spice of religion. Nothing kills religious worship so quickly as monotony. Nothing stifles religion's vitality so completely as being poured into a narrow mold.

St. Paul recognizes that fact in his letters to the Corinthian church. Evidently certain members were trying to confine the enthusiasm of the rest within a narrow groove. At any rate, the apostle felt it necessary to get this conflict between variety and monotony straightened out for his brethren. If we paraphrase his words in the 12th chapter of 1 Corinthians, we find him saying something like this: There are in the church varieties of talent, varieties of service, and varieties of results of the use of talent and service. Some men can preach, others can pray, others teach, and others heal. Some are good at planning and serving church suppers, others at administering charity, others at raising funds, and others at sewing. Yet each one of these talents and services, says the apostle, is the gift of God's spirit, and each is to be used for the common good of all. That is what makes a church vital—when each man and woman, boy or girl, contributes of his God-given ability to the achievement of the common goal. When we put Paul's words into such language it becomes not only intelligible, but a vital bit of advice for any church in any time or place.

Let us see what that advice implies. In the first place, it blasts that exclusiveness of control which always lies in wait for a Christian church. There was no specialized and professional ministry or priesthood in the church at the time Paul wrote this letter. But already there had grown up within the church a small group of leaders who sought to exercise authority. That was inevitable, for no human organization or group can amount to anything without duly constituted authority being entrusted to someone. Paul, the great statesman and organizer, was too wise to overlook that fact. What he did object to was the easy assumption that the church existed primarily as a background for the peculiar talents of its leaders. His objection was on two grounds. In the first place, such thinking tended to make these same leaders believe that the church was their own

Variety, the Spice of Religion

private property; and secondly, it tended to make the rest lazy and indifferent to their own possible contribution to the church's life.

In all candor it must be admitted that such tendencies were not unique within the Corinthian church. Every church since then has had to guard against them. Every parson is always in danger of thinking his parish to be but the length and shadow of his own personality, an institutional tool to serve his own ends. And failing such subtle egotism, he has to guard against the easy danger of allowing all parish activity, all plans and programs, to center on him, to be the product of his brain, and the result of his own feverish activity.

This last is particularly true because the human nature of church members is not one bit different from human nature in other groups. In lodge, club, society, and church the motto of the membership might well be, "let George do it." (George being the master, president, rector or whatever one calls the head of the organization.) Of course it's often George's fault if he lacks the ability to delegate responsibility and encourage varieties of service. But more often it's the very thing the apostle is talking about, the laziness and indifference of most people—"the church of the heavenly rest."

Another implication of this advice of St. Paul is that within the Christian church, all service ranks the same with God. The test of its value is nothing more nor less than this: has he done his best and has she done what she could? One thinks of this often when some well-meaning friend looks at the progress of a parish and compliments the rector on having achieved it. Bless my soul, it isn't the rector who achieves progress in a parish. It isn't the man who preaches or conducts the services to whom we give some high-sounding title that makes a church go. If it is, that church is headed for calamity.

The quality that makes for vitality in a church is a membership in which each individual is making some contribution to the life of the whole body. That is at once the perennial glory of church life and the spice of church activity. Christian corporate life is not a dull and monotonous tracking in a narrow groove. Rather it is the corporate expression of the infinite varieties of personality and talent which abound in any group of human beings. And for this reason, every contribution to the life of the church, be it of hand or heart or brain, is a spiritual contribution.

We need to remember that when we attempt to classify church people on the basis of the kind of thing they do best. How often we hear a person commended for being spiritual, as though spirituality were the sole possession of those who can pray or preach or speak of religion to their fellows. To be spiritual means to have one's life motivated by the indwelling presence of Christ, and if Christ be the motive force in any life, whatever talent that life puts to use for him and his church is a spiritual occupation. The church has

Variety, the Spice of Religion

need of many kinds of gifts in addition to money. It needs singing voices and the musician's fingers; it needs lay evangelists and servers of tables; it needs the brain of the executive and the devotion of those who can take direction.

In conclusion, this advice of St. Paul would have us see behind the variety of expression the one thing we have in common, the ruling guiding spirit of God. Evidently that was what the people of Corinth forgot. And where the cement of the spirit is lacking, the ordered and substantial foundation of a church crumbles into its individual stones, becoming more like a rock pile than a solid wall. The spirit of God is what binds us all together. Without it the corporate life of the church cannot exist. Furthermore, without that spirit, we as individuals must fail in our task as disciples of Christ. After all, is not that the reason why so much of what we do is ineffectual or full of flaws?

Instead of being motivated by the spirit of Christ, we are too often motivated by selfish desire for precedence or self-expression. That cannot be if we are to live effectual Christian lives. It must be for Christ's sake and for our brethren's sake that we live and work. When you go to the altar of your parish church, to that holy meal which nourishes our corporate life, may I ask you to be mindful of two things: first, of the wisdom of God in finding use for the variety of talents of those kneeling at the table with you; and second, of God's need of your own special capabilities if his work is to be done. And in thinking of these two things, may we be especially conscious of his brooding spirit, firing us all to pray and live and work for the common good.

3

The Strenuous Life

THERE have been many kinds of saints in the long history of the church. Some have been seers and others doers. Some have withdrawn from the world and others have gone out into the world. Some, like Mary, loved to sit at the feet of the Christ. And others, like Martha, loved to minister to him.

It all depends upon one's own temperament as to which kind of saint one prefers. The spirit and temper of an age determine what qualities of sainthood are most to be admired, for saints, being real flesh-and-blood persons before they are canonized, tend to reflect in the field of religion the spirit of the age that produced them. Thus the age of the troubadors produced St. Francis, who in his own simple love songs of the faith, epitomized his time. The age of the conquistadors found its religious expression in the stern discipline and aggressive spirit of Ignatius and his Jesuits.

It is not otherwise with the great apostle St. Paul. He was

the product of his own peculiar temperament and the age to which he belonged. In a very real sense, St. Paul was remarkably modern as we rate modernity. He would have been at home in our bustling cities. He would have loved our sports and reveled in the fast tempo of our lives. He would have welcomed the opportunity our age gives to a man of action, because while he had a quick and logical mind, his main concern was in relating the gospel to life as men live it. Paul was no theorist, no walled-in saint enjoying the contemplative life, but a man whose religion had to work or he would have none of it. His world, like ours, required tough-mindedness. It was no place for the squeamish, the timid, or the theorist. And since that was the kind of world in which his lot was cast, Paul was the very kind of man Christ needed to make a dent upon it.

Let us see how God took hold of that man Paul and used his peculiar qualities as an apostle to a strenuous age. Perhaps in so doing we may see how those same qualities can be used in our own strenuous times. The first thing that strikes one as he becomes better acquainted with Paul is his restlessness. Offhand we might say that is no virtue. Certainly, it isn't easy to live with, and when it means nothing more than the rolling-stone temperament, it is about as hopeless a quality as anyone could possess. So I do not mean that Paul was a fidgety, fickle lover of change and novelty. His was the restlessness of the pioneer who was always pressing on to some new adventure for his Lord.

Had he not been that kind of man, he would have been content to stay in Aegeum, even if he had seen the vision of the Greek standing on the far shore of the Aegean crying, "Come over to Macedonia and help us." He would have hesitated, held back, waited for someone else to go. But that was not Paul's way. All his life long it was as though someone were beckoning him on to forsake his friends and settled pastorate and go on somewhere else where hard spadework and planting were to be done. Let other men water the garden of the Lord, cultivate the growing life of the churches and reap the harvest. As for him, give him the task of preparing the soil and sowing the seed.

Even in his last hard years as a prisoner in Rome, his mind was pushing on to Spain and Gaul. He never forgot his old friends, and nowhere in all literature will you find more touching evidences of affection than in his letters, yet he was ever seeking new challenges. One is reminded constantly of his Lord's words, "Foxes have holes, and the birds of the air have nests; but the Son of man has nowhere to lay his head" (Luke 9:58).

Paul's restless spirit manifested itself not only in his travels, but in his thought and in his life. There is just as much progress in his comprehension of the truth that is in Christ as there was in his work. We can see that growth by beginning with his letter to the Galatians and then going on to those to the Corinthians, Romans, Ephesians, and Philippians. Pioneering with Paul was not so much a matter of geography as of the spirit. He was not content to stay in any comfortable little segment of the truth, but rather roamed the universe of the mind in search of it. All his life long he pressed on toward the prize of the high calling of God in Christ Jesus. Yet in the midst of this feverish activity of body, mind, and spirit, the central core of his being was possessed of an infinite calm. His restlessness had purpose in it.

Another characteristic of St. Paul was his intense ardor. It is as though at the center of his being a consuming fire burned. We see that in him before his conversion, when his ruling passion was to stamp out the Christian heresy. Afterwards, that fire which had burned so negatively became intensely positive. Only once in his whole ministry do we find Paul trying to be unimpassioned with his hearers, and that was at Athens, his one and only complete failure. Not one single man was moved toward Christ when he tried to give those sophisticated, logic-shopping Athenians a learned discourse on the nature of God. He found that an intensely emotional age could be moved only by an equal intensity of feeling. His ardor was rooted in complete and selfless devotion to his master. He had been so deeply moved by the sublime tragedy of crucified love that it passed his comprehension how others could not be equally moved. Yet Paul never played upon men's emotions without reference to their thoughts and actions. No one can read his reasoned sentences, or his straightforward practical application of the Gospel to concrete life situations, and say that he was merely an emotional preacher. One is always moved to deep thought and drastic difficult action.

His ardor took still another form, and that was his love of a good fight. He enjoyed slugging it out with an opponent. He fought clean and fair, but he fought, from the moment in Jerusalem when he battled the apostles successfully on the matter of taking uncircumcised Gentiles into the church, to that last time in Jerusalem when he withstood the mob, and standing on his rights as a Roman citizen, told Festus, the proconsul, and Agrippa, the puppet king, exactly what he thought of his opponents in general and themselves in particular. But more important was the eternal battle he and Christ waged within his own soul and body against the power of evil in himself. He describes himself as a boxer, trading blow for blow with his adversary, sometimes losing, but thank God, more often winning the victory with Christ's help. He says this is no shadow boxing, but a real fight in which self-discipline, training, and stamina count.

There is yet one more factor in Paul's character which we must consider, and that is his hard, common-sense, practical approach to religious living. He believed in Christ, not only because of a mystical experience, but because he had the evidence to prove the value of that belief. He saw it first in his own life, in the transformation of the bitter, cruel Pharisee into the "apostle to the Gentiles." He knew what it meant to have hatred turned into love, bitterness into joy, conflict into peace. I doubt very much if Paul would have been obedient to the heavenly vision if all these had not been true. He had seen it work in others, too. That is why so much of his writing is concerned with getting the gospel right down to where people live: in their homes, in their group relationships, in their businesses. The big cities of the Roman empire were like big cities in any age. They are hard places in which to be a Christian. Temptations to revert to sub-Christian standards of living are everywhere. The very noise and bustle and confusion make it difficult for a man to be still and know his God. But if Christianity cannot work in a big city, it has lost the center of life in an age like his or ours. I think you can see why Paul lived so strenuously. He had to, in order to make the gospel real to a strenuous age. His temperament fitted him for it or he would have broken under the strain. But at the heart of his busy life there lay the secret which far eclipsed his temperament. The citadel of his soul was Christ's citadel. The strength of the task was Christ's strength. The purpose of his life was Christ's purpose.

"I can do all things in him who strengthens me" (Philippians 4:13), was not the empty boast of an egotist, but the blunt, glorious fact which he had discovered in being busy for his Lord. It is his kind of sainthood our age needs. His kind of Christianity to which our age will respond. We cannot avoid the strenuous life if we would. But at the core of our restlessness there can be a divine purpose and the inner calm which Christ alone can give. We cannot escape from conflict, but we can equip ourselves for the fight by self-discipline and a clear purpose. God has not given us to lie on beds of ease, but to endure hardship as good soldiers of Jesus Christ. These hardships are not often physical, as they were for Paul. Perhaps we should be better Christians if they were. But it is still true that to follow Christ is no cinch, and if we think it is, we have missed the meaning of discipleship and we shall fail inevitably to win this strenuous, turbulent, brawling generation to the only master able to save it from destruction.

4

Beyond Facts

A SOPHISTICATED modern, considering himself emancipated from the naive faith of the past, has said that "religion is believing in something that you know ain't so." Which really means, I presume, that he thinks that all of us who believe in God are either halfwits or past-masters at the art of self-deception.

Of course, there is that in some religious faiths that gives our sophisticated friend a chance to draw such a conclusion. He can point to the religion of the sentimentalist who acknowledges allegiance to a God or a church simply because his parents did, or because such an allegiance is part of an accepted social code. He can cite those credulous people who keep their religion in an airtight compartment of their minds, never letting the winds of thought, experience, and knowledge blow through the musty corner where faith is stored away. Or he can point to the ease with which man can get his own will, his own desires and ambitions, all tangled up with what he believes to be the will of God, and thus give a religious flavor to the service of self. In these instances, at least, our sophisticated friend's conclusion is valid, and when one whose faith is nothing more than this runs up against a real test, it collapses.

In other and more glorious ways than our sophisticate could ever understand, his conclusion is not valid, and I for one thank God for that. If religion were solely made up of that which one could know as definitely as he knows that two plus two equal four, then religion would lose half its thrill and most of its attractiveness. There is nothing very exciting about that which is cut and dried. I have never seen anyone go into ecstacy over the fact that two apples and two more apples make four apples. Neither could one get very enthusiastic about worshipping a God whose existence was as completely demonstrable as a mathematical formula.

The attractiveness of religious faith grows out of the mystery of life. It has been popular of late to stress the doubt and the fear of man before the unknown and the unpredictable. But doubt and fear are not the only emotions aroused by the mysterious element in life. It attracts us, lures us on, makes us strive to break through the veil, and pierce to the core of its secret. That is true, not only in religions, but in many other areas of human experience. And particularly, it is true when it comes to our experience of other persons. There is a whole lot of truth, for example, behind the vaudeville comedian's thrusts at the failure of most men to understand women. It is a man's attempt, never quite successful, to understand the object of his love which keeps that love firm and strong. Let a man become convinced that he has completely mastered the mystery in his beloved's personality and that man will seek out another mystery to solve, because there is no thrill in an open secret.

Consider the mysterious depths in the growing personalities of children. It is not only the heartache of parenthood which results, but the glorious experience of watching the unfolding of that which always surprises us with its unpredictable variety. Again, it's the mystery of friendship, the occasional and unexpected flashes of some inner quality of mind and spirit, that makes our fellow man so eternally interesting.

So in that relationship between the person of man and the person of God which is the essence of all high religious faith, it is that which we do not know, as much as that which we do know, that keeps the relationship alive. We should become terribly tired and bored with a God whom we completely understood, just as we become bored with other persons whose actions and feelings we can always predict. True, we have to have some permanence, some fundamental and changeless things in any relationship, if it is to endure. We cannot build a love or a friendship on shifting sands. But beyond that, there must be something hidden, something always unfolding yet never completely revealed, if that personal relationship is to remain vital and full of challenge.

Beyond Facts

Such is the relationship between man and God upon which a vital religion can be established and maintained.

How clearly all this is revealed in man's experience with Jesus. Although the four gospels seem to contradict each other in certain ways, there is no indictment of either the truth of Jesus' life and message, or the honesty of the men who wrote the stories. On the contrary, they are proof conclusive that there was in Jesus so much more than any one man or group of men could ever grasp. There still is. And it is our very difficulty in understanding him completely that makes him such an interesting and dynamic person two thousand years afterward. If our doubtful and sophisticated modern wants a God who is thoroughly known and comprehended, or none at all, I am afraid he is asking for something that he can't find. And I, for one, am glad that there is still mystery in the God whom I seek to serve.

In the second place, the statement that religion is believing something you know isn't so, puts its finger quite unconsciously upon another element which is at once the glory and the strength of vital religion, and that is faith. Unfortunately, a lot of people think the difference between knowledge and faith is something like this—two plus two equal four is knowledge; to contend that two plus two equals five, is faith. But that is not faith; that is sheer nonsense and can never be anything other than a travesty on faith.

Faith is, and must be, grounded in that which has been proven true. It is all wrong to suppose that faith is a leap in the dark, with no springboard from which to start and no place to land. For the Christian, faith in God is based upon several things which are facts. Supremely, there is the fact which was and is Jesus Christ. Not only the man born in a stable, reared at a carpenter's bench, and crucified on a cross; not only the human character; but that other Christ whose soul found expression in a life and in words such as no other has lived or spoken; that other Christ who, though men thought him dead, can still command an allegiance more profound than any leader of history. So long as we have him, our faith roots in solid fact.

But faith has another side, and that is its power to make assumptions, its willingness, if you will, to gamble on the implications of the facts already obtained. The whole Christian philosophy of life rests upon such assumptions. It builds upon the fact of Jesus Christ its whole attitude toward God and man. It is not and cannot be unmindful of other facts which seem to point to different conclusions. It must reconcile the conflicting elements of human experience. But in the last analysis, all other facts must, in the faith of a Christian, be subordinate to that supreme fact which is Jesus Christ.

Take, for example, the facts of the story of his trial and death. They are brutally simple and clear, and add up to this: he was mistaken, he failed, he died a tragic death, his enemies won, he lost.

Why is it then, that man has not tried to forget this unhappy event? There is only one reason, and that is the presence in that brutal narrative of something which is above and beyond everything else—the evidence of a divine love. It is love which saves the day on Calvary. It is love which makes of that diabolical record of the perverted souls of men, the one story which man would rather hear than any other ever told. In other words, the divine love revealed in that bitter tragedy is the unseen evidence before which all mere facts fade into insignificance. Behind that evidence, sensed and felt rather than known, lies the sublime assumption that God is our Father. That evidence was the product of Jesus' faith. He didn't lose. He won the only thing that mattered, vindication of his faith in the redemption of you and me.

Therefore, when the cynic tells me that faith is believing what isn't so, in the light of the experience on Calvary, I can answer with confidence. The violence of nature and the strife of a war-torn society are facts which might tell me otherwise. But I happen to know one man who, in his own person, endured all the concentrated wrath man and nature could bring on him. And yet I see in him the triumph of love over hate, of spirit over flesh, of courage over pain, and of life over death. And in the light that streams from Calvary, I learn to distrust all lesser interpretations of the facts of experience that I find in him.

The world needs that sort of faith today. I need it and you need it. It is naive in the way a child is naive. What of it? For did not this same Jesus admonish us to be as little children? So, I say to you, accept the mystery of life with its divine surprises and unsuspected powers as the very key which unlocks the door to a vital relationship with God. Go on to make those sublime assumptions without which life becomes empty and futile, but with which light shines in the darkness and leads us onward with courage and with hope.

5

God's Standard Wage

THE emotions of men are always getting involved with religion. That is inevitable because religion, if it is real at all, is itself a thing of the emotions. Let a human love be shared by religious people and it becomes, in and of itself, a religious expression. That is true of friendship, of the relationship between parents and child, and supremely between a man and a woman. When religion becomes a powerful emotion, it reinforces our whole emotional nature. It heightens the creative imagination of the artist and musician, it gives wings to the hope which springs eternal in human breasts, it becomes inextricably involved in all human loyalties and all human endeavor. By the same token—and herein lies the tragedy of too much religious history—religion can also become involved in some of the devastating emotions which curse rather than bless. It can turn loyalty into a blind sentimentality or a burning intolerance of others' loyalties. It can make men glow with a white-hot hatred, it can foster a spiritual pride which eclipses all other kinds of pride, it can make jealousy and ambition the curse of the ministry, and bolster resentments with a kind of bitterness terrible to behold.

Our Lord recognized all this in the days of his flesh. He had to face it among the twelve on whom he entirely depended. He found religion-bolstered emotion the chief cause of opposition to his gospel from the pious Jews. It is not at all surprising that some of his most powerful parables are aimed at this age-old problem. The story of the prodigal son, which cannot be understood apart from the character of the elder brother, is aimed at the jealousy and resentment which the good often feel toward the bad when the bad are converted. The parable of the laborers in the vineyard is a twin to that of the prodigal son. A farmer goes out at six o'clock in the morning and hires as many as he can find to work in his vineyard at the prevailing wage of twenty cents a day. The grapes were dead ripe on the vine. He went out again at nine, twelve and three o'clock and hired more help. Still the job was not completed. So he went out again at five o'clock and gathered in a few more. When the time came for the men to line up for their pay, those hired last were paid a full day's wage. And so on down the line to those who had worked the full twelve hours. When these found that everyone had received the same wage, they demanded more. When the farmer faced the spokesman for the disgruntled men and asked if he hadn't agreed to pay them twenty cents, the

God's Standard Wage

answer was obvious. He went on to tell them to take what they had earned, and not to use his generosity as an excuse for their meanness.

I am sure you see the parallel between the resentment of those who had borne the heat and burden of the day and that of the elder brother in the story of the prodigal son. And I'm also sure that you, like myself, can understand that resentment. But remember that this is a story of the Kingdom of Heaven. So let us look briefly at what our Lord is saying to us in this story. First, he is recognizing that even in the Kingdom of Heaven, in the church, in any religious task we may share with each other, the common human traits of jealousy, greed, resentment, and the struggle for preferment will crop up. And they will crop up, as I said in the beginning, with a religious motivation. There is no question here about the quality of workmanship of those who worked the longest. It is presumed that they had worked hard and effectively. Laziness and indifference were not their faults, neither are these the faults of many religious people. More than one church has been kept alive by a few bearing the heat and burden of difficult days. But their very loyalty and devotion, tested by years of faithfulness, sometimes leads such people to resent those who are new, those who come in at the eleventh hour and enjoy the same privileges. You will find this in some old well-established parishes where a great gulf is fixed between the old members and the new. You will find it in the subconscious resentment of older branches of Christianity like our own toward the vitality and growth of denominations arriving later on the scene. Yes, I'm afraid it's all part of the Kingdom of Heaven!

More important are some other things in this story. Our Lord is trying to tell us that the relationship between man and God is a contractual relationship. Like the vineyardist, God has a job to be done. The fruit is ripe on the vine; all around us are men and women, young people and children whose lives, like grapes, are ready to be harvested. Like the farmer, God can't do it alone. The task is too great, and again like the farmer, God doesn't care very much who does it or how long one works. The catholic branches of the church have been around for a long time, and still the harvest is not in. The latecomers of Christianity, the protestant denominations, are needed too. The point is, that God has work to be done for which he contracts to pay, not in some coin worth twenty cents, but in the peace and power and joy that come from helping him, and in the grace he confers upon us through worship and sacrament. It is, I say, a contract. We promise God something; he promises us something. We give; and he gives in return. Usually more than we have earned.

Which brings us to the primary thing our Lord is trying to tell us, and that is that no matter how long we have been under contract to God, no matter when we arrived on the scene, no matter how gifted we may be, he has only one thing to give us in return. His is, if you will, a standard wage. A sort of communion of the spirit in which we all get the same thing.

God's Standard Wage

Call it salvation, redemption, eternal life. Call it by any name, theological or otherwise, it is always and everywhere the same. We may not all use what he pays us to equal advantage. Some of us may squander it, some hoard it so it becomes useless, and some invest it wisely. But we cannot escape the egalitarian nature of God's grace. His intention for each is the same. In his vineyard there is only one wage—the gift of God which is eternal life.

So to you who perhaps stood idle in the marketplace for a long time, the Lord says, come, it is not too late to help. Perhaps no one has asked you before, but I am asking you now. Never mind about your capacities and skills, I can give you these. Only come, come now, for I need you. There is still time left before sundown. And to those who have been on the job longer, he says, rejoice with me that these others have come to help, even though late. Don't resent it if they seem to get as much as you. I have only one wage in my Kingdom—the saving grace of God. When I have given you that, I have given you all.

6

Paradoxes

THE Christian religion is, above all else, a religion of paradoxes. It is not surprising that this is so since the life of our Lord is in itself a paradox. That the greatest personality the world has ever known should be born of the wife of a humble carpenter, that a savior should enter the world in a stable, that the first sounds heard by his infant ears should be the lowing of the cattle, the bleating of sheep, and the braying of an ass, makes his life begin in a paradox of humility and greatness.

That contradiction continues in all that we know of his life: The sinless one being tempted in the wilderness as few men are tempted and afterward being baptized with sinners in the Jordan. The carpenter speaking with an authority no scribe versed in the law nor prophets possessed. The gentle Jesus incurring by his very gentleness the violent opposition of the powers that be. The Son of God choosing as his intimates a nondescript band of fishermen. The king with no

Paradoxes

palace, no court, no army, who nevertheless managed and still manages to claim the allegiance of millions though other kingdoms come and go.

No wonder one whose life is as full of contradictions as his should teach in paradoxes—lose your life in order to find it, give in order to get, sorrow in order to know true joy, humble yourself in order to be exalted, and surrender in order to win. It is also no wonder that one whose earthly life was one long paradox should finish his career in the greatest contradiction of all—dying in order to live. There is no significance to the cross without the empty tomb, and none to the tomb without the cross. They are both part of the impossible and unbelievable climax of an impossible and unbelievable life which is nevertheless true as nothing else is true.

There is no point in my attempting to convince you by logic or reasoning that it is fact and not fancy, truth and not myth that brings us here today. The logic is all against it. Forsaken by his friends, misunderstood even by those who knew him best, brutally handled by his enemies, and crucified as a criminal on a Roman cross, Jesus Christ was a defeated man if anyone was ever defeated. He had tried and failed and the failure was the greater because his goal was greater. Where logic takes one in this matter is to a closed tomb of a dead visionary in a lonely garden.

But where logic ends, that which is above logic, which we call by various names—faith, miracles, God—takes over. What happened on Easter day has never been explained nor can it be. However, the tomb was empty, he was not dead but risen. The disciples knew it beyond any shadow of a doubt. The resurrection changed their lives from mediocrity to greatness, from disillusionment to belief, from defeat to victory, and set their once dead, but now living, Lord free from the shackles of time and place to roam the earth with saving power. The conviction that he is not dead but living did and does many things for those who are convinced. But I want to think primarily of what his victory over death does for us.

Let us be honest with each other, most of us are afraid of death. That fear, seldom admitted, lurks within the recesses of our souls and expresses itself in many subtle ways. Partly it is the fear of the unknown, partly the instinct of self-preservation rebelling at ultimate defeat, partly the ego clinging to its tenuous grasp on life and resenting the possibility of annihilation. Much of man's absorption in things, in houses, in bank accounts, in skyscrapers, in business, and in organized religion roots in his attempt to thwart death by holding on more fiercely to what he calls life. Yet strangely enough, the more man fears death, the more he seems to court it. Such is the perversity of our natures. Many who throw themselves into business or politics or the amassing of wealth in the attempt to forget their mortality, die of heart attacks in their prime. Many who become overly concerned about their health wind up as neurotics whose imaginary ills tend, with time, to become real and fatal. The Christian religion would not have survived all these centuries if it had not helped men to overcome that fear, if it had not shown us the way to conquer our last and greatest enemy. And it does so because of our Lord's conquest of death.

In the first place, the resurrection of Jesus shows us that the death of his body has nothing whatsoever to do with all that makes human personality what it is. Being creatures of earth, that is no easy lesson for us to learn. The beauty of the earth on a clear day or when clouds pile up high above the mountains, the sight of the familiar things that make home home, the sound of a loved one's voice, the clasp of a friend's hand, the thrill of seeing the work of one's life bear fruit—all are fine, substantial, real things that make life on this earth what it is. They are things we have known in the body and we can't separate them from the body. I'm sure these things were part of what our Lord was loath to give up when he prayed in the garden that night before his death.

Yet, it is not man's body that makes all these things so precious. It is his spiritual capacity which makes him see the beauty of the earth, and it is his ability to love that makes the clasp of a hand and the sound of a voice so meaningful. It is his capacity for thought and purpose and will which makes the work of his life so interesting. And none of these things is physical; they all belong to that mysterious part of our nature which, for want of a better word, we call the soul. They express themselves in and through the body, but they are not of the body. And when the body dies, it is not the empty corpse we remember, but that which inhabited it and gave it life.

So whatever else the resurrection of Jesus may have meant to his disciples, I am sure what mattered most was the conviction that his love, his moral power, and his divine purpose were not dead. Had his resurrected body been all-important, they could not have carried on after he appeared to them for the last time. Were it all-important now we should not be concerned. The empty tomb and the resurrection appearances were only God's way of leading earthbound men above the physical to the realm of the spirit which knows no limitations of the flesh. That is why we can believe he is alive today and forever more. We need no more convincing proof than the timelessness of his message, the presence of his spirit in our lives, and the inability of succeeding generations of evil men to destroy his grip on the human soul. Therefore, when we affirm at Easter that he has destroyed death by dying, we mean that he has destroyed death's awful finality, its grim power, and its seeming disregard for the precious qualities of human personality.

But this does not mean that we are automatically covered by the blanket insurance of his deathlessness. The Christian doctrine of the resurrection is too easily confused with the pagan doctrine of immortality, that sentimental assumption that all men, no matter what the quality of their lives, are automatically guaranteed entrance into the land of light and joy at the moment of death. However much we may wish this were so, there is nothing in the New Testament to back it up.

So if you would not fear death, the overcoming of that fear roots in your having known increasingly, as the years go by, his vital living presence in your life. His conquest of death begins the moment we place our lives under his control and take him truly as our Lord and master. It grows as we grow in his knowledge and love. But the conquest of man's greatest and last enemy is a campaign of years and not a battle of one final moment. It involves beating down the assaults of the world, the flesh, and the devil. It includes putting off the old things which are the bane of our mortal life: pride, jealousy, hatred, lust, covetousness; and putting on the new things which bless: humility, charity, self-control, purity, generosity.

The Easter collect speaks of the risen Christ opening to us the gate of eternal life. It is a narrow gate at the end of a straight road. We must reach that gate and walk through it ourselves. But always there is at our side one who knows the way because he has been there before us. We may limp a bit as we reach the gate and bear in our bodies the scars of the long campaign. But that, in itself, is a certification that we have, through his grace, gained the victory and the "well done" of the master inviting us in to dwell with him forever.

7

The Sacraments

WHEN we think of the various means by which God makes his grace available to us, we must consider the supreme importance of the sacraments. In the view of the Episcopal church there are two chief sacraments necessary to salvation: baptism, by which one is made a child of God and a member of his Church; and the Lord's supper or holy communion, whereby the life begun in baptism is nourished and sustained throughout one's earthly life.

There are five other rites which the church performs on special occasions which are sacramental, although less important than the two chief sacraments. These so-called lesser sacraments are confirmation, holy matrimony, holy orders, penance or the absolution of sins, and unction of the sick. Why are these acts which the church performs so important? What do they give to others which can be given in no other way? In other words, why do we call these the chief means of grace?

The Sacraments

We must begin our attempt to answer these questions by examining God's problem in reaching us. He is infinite and we are not. He is spirit and we are flesh. He is limited by nothing except his love, while we are bound to earth, surrounded by matter, engulfed in the hard necessity of making material things serve our needs. If God is to reach us at all, he must, among other ways, do so through our senses, and therefore through material things. Since our life is made up of touching, hearing, seeing, tasting, and smelling the material environment in which we live, it is by these avenues that the creator must come to us. And since he is the creator of matter as well as spirit, he uses matter to break through to us in the sacraments.

But we have a problem. Born as creatures of earth, we yet bear within us a potential hunger for that which is above and beyond earth. We are, as is so often said, creatures of two worlds, both earth and heaven, and all our lives long we endure the inevitable struggle between these two sides of our nature. Therefore, the only possible way by which this conflict can be resolved is by somehow bringing both earth and heaven, matter and spirit, together in some possible fusion of the two so that the claim of earth upon us does not choke or starve or kill our hunger for God. Such is our human problem.

Here then is the essential realism which lies at the heart of Christian worship. Christianity, as Dr. Schweitzer has said, is the most materialistic religion known to man. It is not afraid of using material things to express spiritual things; rather, it takes the stuff of earth, simple things like water, bread, wine and oil, or the more complex things which man fashions out of metal, wood, and glass and finds in them the means whereby God speaks to us of heaven, and the means by which we climb upward toward him on a ladder made out of the products of this earth. It is this which the old definition of a sacrament in the catechism seeks to express. "A sacrament is the outward and visible sign of an inward and spiritual grace given unto us; ordained by Christ himself, as a means whereby we receive the same, and a pledge to assure us thereof" (*Book of Common Prayer*, 1928).

As this classic definition so clearly states, it is from Christ we get the sacramental insight so important not only to our worship, but to our very life itself. It is from his frank grasping of the problem that Christian man has learned the secret of using the things of earth to express his hunger for heaven. Matter is neither good nor evil in Jesus' teaching. It is man's understanding and use of it which makes it good or evil. The sacramental approach to life has as its goal, not only the suffusing of the material by the spiritual, but the redeeming of the material from base animal usage to that which leads man upward toward God.

Looking now more specifically at the meaning of the sacraments, let us recognize that religion's use of material symbols for spiritual things is by no means a monopoly. Old Glory fluttering in the breeze, as every patriot knows, is something more than colored cotton bunting. We respect the flag because of what it stands for, not because it is a pretty rag. The bill you put on the offering plate is something more than a piece of engraved paper. A nation's currency stands for the integrity of its government and the soundness of its economy; it is an outward and visible sign of intangible and tangible things we gladly offer to God. It is the inward and spiritual value which is important in a gift to a friend. So it is with a multitude of things we use to express something more than their material value.

We see this same principle working in the lesser sacraments of the Church which Christ accepted from the common religious practices of mankind. The laying on of hands by the bishop in confirmation and ordination is but the outward sign of the Church's desire to pass on to others what she has received at the hands of God and her Lord. The exchange of a ring in holy matrimony is more than a pretty, sentimental, and socially acceptable bit of ritual, or it isn't holy matrimony. The purpose is the same: that in and through these symbolic acts, the grace of God needed for each state and relationship of life may be given to those involved.

But it is in the two symbolic acts which Christ specifically asks us to perform that this fusion of matter and spirit takes on its highest meaning. Jesus did not invent the sacrament of baptism. Its symbolic use was at least a hundred years old when he was baptized in the Jordan by John the Baptist. But

Jesus took it and gave it a new and greater significance far beyond the symbolic cleansing from sin. The outward and visible sign of cleansing water still remains, as does the need of repentance. But baptism becomes the sign of a new birth into the life of God's family, the Church. It is enlistment as Christ's faithful soldier and servant until life shall end. It is the badge of one's claim upon eternal life. More important, it is the assurance that God will do his part to guarantee all these things to us if we try to live up to what we said or what was said in our name at our baptism. It is also the assurance that God knows our name, that we have a unique claim upon him as every child has upon his father. And that we are, therefore, not lost.

In the sacrament of the altar our Lord takes the sacred Passover meal of the Jews and gives it a new and more sublime significance. He himself becomes the outward and visible sign in terms of our humanity and God's love and grace. He uses the simple elements of unleavened bread and table wine to make us see what his own sacramental offering means. There is something so unutterably simple and unspectacular in what he did in the upper room on the night before his death. Just a few words of blessing, the breaking of bread, and the sharing of the cup with the simple command to take and eat for this is his body, and to drink for this is his blood. And then the final exhortation to remember him always whenever bread and wine are shared by Christian people.

The Sacraments

Mind you, there was no fuss, no ringing of bells, no blaring of trumpets, no gorgeous vestments, but only the snap of breaking bread, the gentle earthy sound of sipping lips, the psalm sung before they left, and the plain clothing of countrymen in that plain bare room. And yet in that simplicity there lay such a profound meaning as to escape man's comprehension through all time. No wonder we call the re-enactment of that scene a holy mystery! No matter how we may in our worship overlay its simplicity with the elaborate trimmings of a festival celebration, the simplicity and the mystery remain to haunt and move us as nothing else we ever do.

Here then we see the sacramental means of grace at its highest and best. That there is danger in such realism no one dare deny, and a church which places a high value on it must always be on guard lest the symbols become more important than that which they symbolize. Idolatry is never very far away from the sacramentalist. If he becomes too engrossed in the outward and visible signs, the inward and spiritual grace cannot get through.

At no time in the year are we reminded of this constant danger more than in Holy Week. The crosses are veiled, the altars are unadorned, the holy communion services are quiet and simple and given over largely to the constant repetition of the story of the cross. On Good Friday all symbols are removed, and the church becomes as bare as a meeting house that we may concentrate upon nothing but his passion. Then having restored our balance and heeded the great simplicities, on Easter day we worship with all we have to offer of splendor and joy. Such is the sound realism of a sacramental approach to God, an approach which, if it really possesses our souls, can make all material things serve the purpose of the living God seeking to make himself known to us men.

8

Doubt As Faith's Servant

FLIP a coin into the air and it comes up heads or tails. It's the same coin either way it falls, but its meaning depends on how one calls it.

Life is very much like a flipped coin and so is our religion. Jesus recognized this so clearly in such paradoxical statements as "by losing his life for my sake, he will gain it" (Matthew 10:39). And the greatest paradox of all is the final one of his own earthly career, dying on the cross in order that his gospel and his spirit to make the gospel work might go on to the end of time.

The great paradox of the forty days following his resurrection is the interplay of doubt and faith. Like the two sides of the coin, first one, then the other, comes up in the brief words we have of what happened. But it is in that interplay of the human capacity both for doubting and for believing that the story works out to its final conclusion. Throughout the long history of Christianity a premium has been put on faith, and rightly so. St. Paul says it is by faith that we are saved and not by any of the motions we go through in formal worship or in doing good deeds. St. James says that it is faith which enables us to be patient and victorious in temptation. He even goes so far as to say that you are tempted in order that you may see faith at work. If, perhaps, you doubt some of that belief, then I ask you to listen carefully to what I am about to say.

What is often overlooked is that doubt plays a very important part in the achievement of Christian faith. It may not be faith's twin, but it certainly can be faith's servant, and without it faith cannot be what it must be. Faith is essential if we are to understand the pressures of our existence.

All during the brief months of Jesus' ministry, we see the faith of the disciples growing out of their doubt. At first they followed him because they liked him and he needed them. He offered them an escape from the dull routine of their working lives. He gave them an excuse to go places and to see things they had always wanted. Further, he believed in them in spite of the frightful inadequacies of all of them. But they hadn't the remotest idea of who he was other than a carpenter of Nazareth. They raised questions as to his strange new teachings and often, when he explained, they still didn't understand. Ever and again they doubted his wisdom and power. When, near the end, he asked them who they thought he was, they frankly didn't know. Perhaps he was Elijah come to life, or John the Baptist. It was only after persistent

Doubt As Faith's Servant

pressure that Peter blurted out, "thou art the Christ." But afterwards, he didn't really believe it.

After the tomb was found empty their doubts were stronger than ever. Even those who came by faith naturally had to be convinced. Women often find faith easier than men, but even Mary Magdelene, who loved him deeply, did not stop sorrowing until he spoke her name. Peter, who had once half believed that Jesus was the Christ, evidently alternated between doubt and faith more than once. It was not until the risen Lord confronted him on the shore of Galilee that he finally came to an unwavering conviction. Thomas was not the only doubter; he was simply the most intelligent one. They all had difficulties believing Jesus was alive. The faith they finally achieved was hard to reach, and the slippery steps by which they climbed were their doubts.

Faith acquired in this hard way does several things. First, it provides a growing hedge for Christian life and experience. Faith which has all the answers becomes sterile, hard, dogmatic, and dead. It does not know how to face change and new knowledge and new experience. Faith must be open-ended enough to accept and deal with new truths, to experiment, to test, and to grow in the process. In other words, there must be room in our faith for healthy agnosticism which frankly admits it does not know all the answers and has not learned all the truths, and yet is not afraid to seek them. Such a faith is not blind acceptance of something we think should be believed, nor does it shut out those who do not agree with us in every detail.

Second, such a faith is a lifetime process rather than an achievement of a single moment. Paul is often cited as an example of sudden conversion. But he was not. The process by which he moved from bitter doubt to faith began when he stood coldly by at the martyrdom of Stephen, and from his letters we can see his faith expanding until his own death in Rome. The Paul of his early letters still has a lot of the old Phariseeic dogmatizing. He could not have written that matchless 13th chapter of 1 Corinthians, where he puts love more important than faith and stronger than hope at the heart of things, until he had learned it the hard way. His faith, like the disciples', begins with commitment to Jesus Christ, but the meaning of that commitment grows with experience.

Finally, such a faith, while built on the natural human capacity to believe in something or someone, is no self-sufficient virtue apart from other qualities which give it direction. I would remind you that the greatest examples of faith on the grand scale in our century have been the belief of the communists in Marx and Lenin and the belief of the nazis in Hitler.

As I read the gospels and the rest of the New Testament, I find a faith that is strong because it is always brought into context with the love of Christ, without which it can be the most cruel and diabolical thing in all this world. Faith can and does move mountains. But without love such power can curse the life of man and thwart the purposes of God. It is

Doubt As Faith's Servant

only a faith with an open end, with a margin for growth, and a plea for doubt that can find room for love. Without love, faith cannot claim to be Christian.

After all these years in the ministry, I know this is true. As a young man I committed myself to this awesome task almost against my will. Often I feared the shallowness of my faith was in inverse proportion to the dogmatism with which I stated it. But I know now that there never was a time when I knew all the answers, nor do I have them now. Yet one of the joys of this time of life is to know this is so, and to go on trying to find them. The deepest certainties accumulated over the years have not come easily, nor do they now. But at least there is zest to this quest and a certainty in its convictions which make life more interesting than ever. I know that Jesus lives, that he is my patient friend, that he feels the same way about you, and that he gives each of us a hard job to do which involves risk and danger and adventure and the possibility of defeat. I know that he will not do violence to my personality, and that he wants me to be myself. I have bet my life on him, and over the years that gamble has paid off far beyond my greatest hopes. This I believe. Lord, help my unbelief.

9

Life Is a Quest

"AND ye shall seek me and find me, when ye shall search for me with all your hearts" (Jeremiah 29: 13–14).

Life is a quest. From the first cry of the newborn babe, to the last whisper of the dying, man is a seeker after the key to life's mystery. In a very real sense, we are all seeking the Grail, as truly as did Arthur's knights in the dawn of English history. At times we are all lured by a vague uneasiness, a divine discontent with things as they are; the lure of the unknown overwhelms us and we press out into new paths and new adventures.

The frontiers of earth have fallen before the intrepid valor of man. In a sense, we are less fortunate than our fathers. When economic, social, or religious environments became unbearable for them, the beckoning frontier lured them on to the possibility of new successes. They left the unbearable behind and journeyed westward in search of new environments. Now the frontier is gone. That is why the present period of distress is so much more baffling than any of its predecessors. We are forced to sit amidst the ruins of the past because there simply is no new land to which we may escape. In the past, periods of disaster gave man new impetus for adventure. Today our discontent is bottled up within us and we waste its emotional drive in whining fears and complaining criticism.

Because the adventures of the pioneer are closed to us, we are in danger of losing the values our discontent might produce. Whipped on by fear of the unknown future, we are tempted to enclose ourselves and our social systems in a fear-born conservatism which closes its eyes to sin and bulwarks itself in rigid adherence to accepted standards. To do that is to fly in the face of the record of history. Both nations and men who have faced the unknown like cringing cowards, who have entrenched themselves behind things as they are, have perished. To stand still is to die. To advance is to live.

Our times call for courage. They call for men and women of adventurous spirit who are more afraid of standing still than of the uncertainty of the dark unknown. We need to subject our civilization and its institutions to searching scrutiny and constructive criticism. Unless we are possessed by a powerful misgiving which makes us uncertain of many things our fathers and ourselves have taken for granted in other days, the opportunity of the present hour shall pass us by.

This same tendency to reaction is to be found in religion. The restless, eager quest for a new faith and a new God is in danger of spending itself in the frantic return to forsaken paths. The trend in religion is as conservative as the trend in politics. In spite of the vitality of various religious movements, many of them are completely reactionary in their points of view. A return to vital faith is all to the good, but we dare not return to a faith whose outlook is totally unaware of all the new knowledge and insight of our times.

The snug little universe of our fathers is gone. Under the spur of science, we have discovered new infinities within and without, and these new truths have made traditional religion inadequate. To return to old moorings is impossible. But we can believe in a better world, we can attain a new and profound conviction that life is filled with a purpose and a value beyond our ken. And through it all, we catch glimpses of a God who is the God of every seeker, in whose "presence there is fullness of joy," and in whose "right hand are pleasures for evermore" (Psalms 16:11).

There are some things about life as an adventurous quest which I would mention. In the first place, it is necessary for us to fix our goal. Consider these adventurous men. Abraham was in search of a land to the west where he might cease his roaming and settle down with his flocks and herds in a place he could call his own. Moses led the people of Israel out of Egypt in search of the promised land. St. Paul had Rome, and even distant Spain as his objective. Attila led his hordes of

Huns to the treasures of Rome. Columbus sailed west to find a passage to the mystic wealth of the Orient. The pioneer travelled three thousand miles to find the hidden yellow dust of the Sierras. Every one of these men had some one place he wanted to reach more than all others.

Not all of them succeeded. Moses died on the borders of Palestine. St. Paul languished in a Roman prison without seeing the sunny slopes of Andalusia. Columbus discovered the West Indies instead of the East. Those are the risks of human adventure. But all along the road there are blessings as well as hardships. We pick up new experiences as we journey. We learn new facts about tides and winds and currents, new methods of travel, new means of defense against the enemy.

Nor can we minimize the temptations to loiter on the way. Many a pioneer has been lured aside from the main quest by weariness or the ease and comfort of some wayside station. The history of the human race is full of incidents which show how easily our efforts may be deflected from the one clear purpose our youth had formed. And one of the tragic consequences of this satisfaction with something less than the best, is the inevitable decay of personality which only the adventurous life prevents. The fleshpots of Egypt paralyzed the ethical and religious progress of the Hebrews, and in their example we find the tragic parable of the failure of the life from which the questing spirit has departed.

It is like that in our search for God. If security, pleasure or the things he can give us are what we want, we will never find him. St. Augustine was right when he said, "Thou has made us for Thyself, and our hearts are restless until they find rest in Thee." There are countless bypaths luring us aside. A seemingly hostile universe will thwart our hopes and bear us many weary miles off our course. We will doubt the wisdom of the quest, and wonder if the object is real, anyway. But give up, we cannot. And if, perchance, we die before the goal is reached, we may from the high eminence of that great adventure, catch some glimpse through the mist of that toward which we have journeyed. And that will suffice until we awake in the presence of him whose we are.

Another thing about this search for God is its solitariness. Most of the great adventures of life are made alone, or at best, with a few whose purpose is as ours. And it is this loneliness of the quest for God that makes the achievement possible. Nowhere is this truth more clearly portrayed than in Francis Thompson's *Hound of Heaven*. He sought in company of man and maid, in the laughter and tears of little children, the goal of his restless life, only at last to find, "All things betray thee, who betrayest me." And through the powerful cadences of that epic of the questing soul there runs the theme of a loneliness that is deeper than comprehension until it finds the achievement.

We may search the storehouse of literature, we may pry within the secrets of test tube, microscope, and telescope.

There we shall find God. We may clasp to our hearts the beauty of sea and sky, the gentle murmur of the brook, the cool deep shade of the forest. We may stand in awe before the masterpieces of art, or thrill at the elemental expressiveness of great music, and wherever we find beauty, there we shall find God. We may behold the greatness of human character, the sweet naive responsiveness of the child, the tender selfless love of a mother, the deep and sturdy character of men, and wherever we find goodness, there we shall find God. Even in the tragedy of life, the questing soul finds other arrows pointing toward God. The sublimity of man in his agony points to the sublimity of God in his agony, the tragic, awesome beauty of the cross.

So to the quest, Christian people. Be not satisfied with anything less than God. And if, on the upward road, death overtakes you, may it be said of you, as it was said of the Alpine explorer who died in the snows, "he died climbing."

10

The Will to Believe

WHEN we come to church on Easter, each in his own way seeks to express one of the deepest motives of men—the will to believe. It is essential that each of us believe in something or someone other than one's self. Be it the stability of our economic system, the integrity of our government, the work which we do, or more personally, the loyalty of our friends and the love of our families, man must believe in something in order to survive.

The will to believe is focused at Easter on the mystery of Christ's resurrection. For some the focus is blurred, vague, and uncertain beyond a common earthy feeling of spring within our hearts. Others come wistfully wishing to find some adequate answer to that need to believe, yet fearing that there be no answer. Still others, with the certainty of a proven faith, know the fulfillment of that will to believe through song and prayer and sacrament. In other words, churches are crowded on Easter day for none of the reasons cynical people are apt to give. Every last one of us has in his heart the desire for faith, which on this day at least, impels us to come to the house of God hoping to find some response beyond our human contriving to satisfy our soul's hunger. Therefore it behooves us to seek a meaning behind our keeping of this feast and seek it with all our hearts.

Sometimes I wonder if even the convinced Christian realizes how much that what religion has to offer depends upon the truth of Christ's resurrection. Steeped as we are in the modern emphasis upon the Christian way of life, it doesn't often occur to us that the very validity of that way of life rests not upon the precepts and attitudes which our Lord lays down in his parables, but rather upon the sublime fact that the way, exemplified in his person and sealed by his blood, could not be conquered by death. Thus, in his empty tomb, we find the proof of the validity of his claims upon us.

St. Paul, whose life was devoted to the Christ who died and yet lives for evermore, puts it all in one clear dynamic proposition. "If," he said, "if Christ was not raised, your faith has nothing in it . . . " (1 Corinthians 15:12). In other words, apart from the fact of his resurrection and his living spirit moving in the hearts of men, there is nothing to Christianity, nothing at all. So, as we attempt to answer our question, what does his resurrection mean for us, let us examine Paul's statement. If Christ be not risen from the dead, then is your faith in the importance of ideals in vain? It is no secret to any thoughtful person alive in this troubled century that an age like ours is pretty hard on ideals. One by one we've seen standards of truth and purity, of justice and goodwill, of honor and integrity, shrugged off by the cynical or mowed down by the brutal realist. In what has happened to family life, to politics in government, to relations between groups and between nations, ideals are compromised or flaunted with vigor and disdain. When anyone dares stand up for ideals, either he's called a sentimental fool or looked upon as a dangerous character.

Ours might be called an age of crucifixion—crucifixion of morality, of high standards of character, of unselfish goodwill, and selfless love. It is altogether too easy for us to become as cynical about the validity of these things we were once taught as it was for the disciples when their Lord hung limp on Calvary's cross. Our ideals sometimes seem as dead as he seemed. But at just that moment when we are apt to give up, we are confronted with an empty tomb and a risen Christ starting his march through the ages, and proving to the cynical and despairing that ideals which are real and of God and in harmony with his purpose, are never dead for long. Their eclipse at the hands of those pseudoheroes of our times, the realists, is like an eclipse of the sun, but a transitory darkening. The shadow passes, the light breaks forth again. The chill and darkness depart because he lives.

If Christ be not risen from the dead, then is your faith in God's forgiveness in vain? Christian thought and experience has always associated forgiveness of sin with the cross. And rightly so. No honest man, thinking of the cross, can escape feeling he had some part in putting Jesus there. Yet if the cross were all there were to our Lord's act of redemption, all we should see is the bitter tragedy which our sin inflicted. And in killing Jesus, the lover of our souls, we should go through life with sin's burden made heavier because of what we had done to him.

But the empty tomb and the risen Christ cancel all that. The burden of sin repented of, rolls away because the stone which seals his grave is rolled away. Our sin, deadly as it may be, both to ourselves and to the Son of God, is not deadly enough to kill the one who mediates forgiveness. In triumphing over death, he triumphs over the thing that killed him—your sin and mine as well as Peter's and Pilate's, the unthinking mob's, and the Roman soldiers'. He still triumphs over it every time a sin-sick soul brings his burden to him in penitence and faith. For without a living Christ, there can be no forgiveness.

Finally, if Christ be not risen from the dead, then is your faith in immortality in vain? I'm well aware of the fact that people of other religions, or of no religion, bask in a sort of optimistic belief that this life is not all, but in all honesty I must confess that such a belief, apart from Jesus' resurrection, would leave me unmoved. I could not believe it, were it not for the fact that his living presence gives me a different perspective on what we call death than I could have otherwise. More than the protest of the ego against annihilation, more than a feeble whistling to keep one's courage up, more even than a natural human desire to meet again with those we have loved and lost, the Christian belief in the resurrection of the dead and the life of the world to come rests upon a simple fact. He lives; he is risen indeed! And insofar as we are in him and he in us, we are sharers in that deathless life and partakers of his immortality. While such a faith does not remove the inevitable fact of death, it does shake off the fear of its finality. Such a faith enables us to live each day as though it were our last without being morbid about it, but with a trust and joy which only Christ can give.

These then are the resurrection's answers to my need to believe. There are things in the resurrection story and the gospel which often tax my credulity, and certainly pass my poor human comprehension, but there is no question in my mind whatsoever that Christ lives. I have never seen him as the disciples saw him after he arose, no voice has ever spoken in my ear as St. Paul heard him speak from the Damascus road, but I know he is here because there is no explanation within myself for what the likes of me can do and be when I let my will to believe he is alive take possession of me. I am certain of this, also, because the low, mean, un-Christian moments I have known, alas, have always been those when I let that will to believe grow dull within me.

As long as that faith in the living Christ gives me courage to go on believing in truth and honor, in goodness and love, as things worth striving for no matter what others think, as long as his risen presence removes from my shoulders the burden of sin and holds before me the opportunity for new and better living, as long as his conquest of death gives me hope of eternal life, then I must feel that there is none other than Jesus Christ to whom I can give all my needs to believe.

This is the faith I must share with you on Easter. It is a jubilant faith, one which instinctively makes one sing, and gives wings to the soul as nothing else does or can. But it is a faith I can no more hug to myself than could the disciples and the women in that garden long ago. Share it with me, I beg of you. I dare you to live as though he were alive and see what happens. And when you find the gamble of your faith has paid off, as it is bound to do, you will not only wonder why in the world you didn't make that gamble before, but you too will want to share it, even as I must this holy day. Nothing less than the risen Christ and faith in him can give to your need to believe an object worthy of your best devotion.

TWO

God did not give us a spirit of timidity, but a spirit of power and love and self-control.
2 Timothy 1:7

11

The Human Moses

WITH the life of Moses we move out of the earlier folklore in the Bible into the beginnings of Hebrew history. As is always the case in the long history of man, the rise of strong cultural and social institutions is the result of strong leadership. It was Moses who took an enslaved people out of Egypt and laid the foundations, not only of the Hebrew nation, but of the great religious and moral tradition of which Christianity is the legitimate heir.

Next only to our Lord, we owe more to this genius of the ancient world than to anyone else. In common with many great leaders, Moses stands forth in the record of the Old Testament as an aloof and forbidding personality. He's a stern man; fearless, honest, and at times ruthless. He was an indomitable man who, in the face of obstacles which would have defeated a lesser person, persisted for forty years until he could die in peace knowing his objective was in sight.

Yet there is another Moses than the stern, inflexible,

law-giving strategist; a human Moses whose life story is worth recalling. Moses got a favorable start in life at the insistence of a clever mother. The story of the way in which she left her infant son floating in a basket on the Nile, on the chance that he might be discovered by a noble Egyptian, is a story we all have loved from childhood. It took courage for that Hebrew woman to fly in the face of all a mother's instincts in order that her son not be a slave as his fathers had been for three generations. To be sure, she was thinking only of his personal welfare, but in her self-sacrifice lay the seed of freedom for her people.

Brought up in Pharaoh's household as the beloved adopted son of Pharaoh's daughter, we see Moses grow to young manhood in the environment of the court, learning the very arts of government which he would need later on, and securing the broad knowledge of an educated Egyptian. Yet there smoldered within this young man a passion for freedom and a hatred of oppression. Where many a man would have traded on his good luck and used it to feather his own nest, Moses could not. Seeing the Egyptian overseer abusing a Hebrew slave in the brickyard one day, his temper flared white-hot, and before he knew it, the overseer was dead and he was running away from certain punishment which even a prince could not escape under Egyptian law.

Moses' great problem, all his life long, was his temper. He always lost it under intense provocation, as when he smashed the tables of the law on finding his people worshipping the

The Human Moses

golden calf. The Bible tells us that the reason God didn't permit him to enter the promised land was because of his ungovernable temper. Thus, early in the story of the Hebrews, we find God concerned with this common fault of impatient men. A passion for freedom is fine, but when it results in violence, the freedom is lost both for oneself and those he seeks to help. Therefore, we find the former prince a shepherd in the desert of Midian. It was a long hard school Moses attended in that desert, yet God did not let die within him the passion for his people's freedom. Out of the vision of the burning bush came the impetus to return to Egypt and lead his people out of slavery.

It was not an easy assignment nor did Moses feel qualified to undertake it. For there lay at the heart of this seemingly strong man, a deep sense of inadequacy, a saving humility, which was an integral part of his greatness. It was this humility which fostered his complete dependence upon God for guidance and strength. And it was his sense of inadequacy which prompted him to create a staff of helpers and display his genius for organization. All of this he had to find out in the desert of his humiliation. Out of that desert came one of the great leaders of history; not born, but made by God's grace to turn his liabilities into assets.

The outline of the rest of his history is known to most of us. His frustrating and fruitless negotiations with Pharaoh, the seven plagues which fell upon Egypt, the dramatic escape across the Red Sea whose winds and tides to this day, in the shallow northern part, are so capricious that one might walk across at one moment and drown the next. Then there follow those long years of wandering, moving from oasis to oasis, at times nearly dying of thirst and hunger, harrassed by other wandering tribes, plagued by rebellion and disunity, stranded in the hot Arabian peninsula of Sinai. No leader in history had a more difficult people to manage or greater obstacles to overcome. Small wonder that Moses' patience wore thin and his heart grew discouraged. But he never gave up. Sustained by the God whom he had met on the mount, he carried on with a fortitude and wisdom matched by few in all history. How much of the story is history and how much folklore, we do not know, but the outlines of his character are clear. What we see behind the stern, aloof, forbidding facade is a man meeting frustration, defeat, and disillusionment, and yet going on to one fixed goal—the land which God had promised to his people.

The picture of the aging Moses, as the Hebrews come to the border of the promised land, is one of the most moving in all literature. It is said of him that his eye was not dim nor his vital force abated. What a tribute to an old man. As he stands on a high point of land, looking out upon the lush pastures of Canaan clothed in their springtime green, with the olive trees and grape arbors climbing in stately rows up the hills, he does not bemoan the fact that it is Joshua, not he, who shall lead his people to their goal. He has given his life to them, and if they arrive, that is all that matters. Nor does he fear the reports of well-fortified enemies who must be overcome by Joshua and his people before the land is theirs. He has seen God's handiwork in too many crises of the past to doubt his help now.

The greatness of Moses becomes quite clear at the end of his history as nowhere else. He does not think of himself as the indispensable man; he has done the best he could to pick the right leadership to succeed him. He trusts that leadership and he does not fall to those twin curses of age, the harboring of rootless regrets or pessimism about the future. The reason he died old in years, but young in heart, is that he had confidence in his God.

Here was a man made great, not only by his own capacities, but by his absolute trust in the greatness and goodness of God. So alone on the mountain, with the unattained goal within sight, he died happy, content, confident in the future of his people. They never found his body. There was no grave. But no man in history could have a finer epitaph than the simple words, "and Moses was not, for God had taken him."

12

Parables of the Kingdom

JESUS was a master storyteller. Most of his stories are short, drawn from life as his listeners knew it, and illustrative of the realistic insight he possessed of the ways of God and man. Because we've heard them so often, it comes as something of a surprise to read in the gospels that his own disciples had trouble understanding them, and that he had to take time to analyze and explain their meaning. However, I am not sure that his present disciples are any cleverer. The trouble may be that the stories are too familiar, and hearing them over and over again induces a spiritual deafness every bit as profound as that which Jesus meant when he quoted from Isaiah, "'You shall indeed hear but never understand, and you shall indeed see but never perceive. For this people's heart has grown dull, and their ears are heavy of hearing, and their eyes have closed, lest they should perceive with their eyes, and hear with their ears, and understand with their heart, and turn for me to heal them.'"(Matthew 13:14). After fifty years of preaching, of rehearsing again and again the profoundly simple truth Jesus would have us learn, I think I can understand just a bit of the frustration Jesus knew. Yet I keep on trying in his name.

Turning to Jesus' parables, what is our Lord saying to us? What does it mean in terms of our own lives? First, it is important for us to realize that while these are analogies taken from life, we must not be fooled by their simplicity. We make a great mistake in thinking that profound truth must always be stated complexly. Quite the contrary. God speaks to us in the simple experiences of daily living which we overlook or ignore because they are so obvious. This is the glory of Jesus' gospel. It is not cloaked in mystery, it is not esoteric, it does not get lost in speculations about heaven. It deals with earthy things, common experiences, practical wisdom. It would bid us seek heaven in the midst of our mortal life. And it would enable us to find heaven within us as we journey from birth to the grave. How clear all this is in these three parables of the Kingdom of Heaven.

In the first, Jesus takes a realistic approach to the strange and often troublesome mixture of good and evil which characterizes human life. He uses an analogy which the farmers listening to him would understand. A good farmer is always careful about the seed he plants. It must be from good stock with a high yield to justify the labor involved in sowing and reaping the harvest. So he sows his field and goes to bed, tired but content. But, as he sleeps, an enemy under cover of darkness sows other seed in the same field. When the new life begins to show above the ground there are weeds growing among the wheat. His hired hand goes to the farmer, perplexed by the weeds. The farmer seems strangely calm about all of this and very realistic. An enemy has sown those seeds, he says, and when his men suggest a massive weeding operation, the farmer says, "No, lest in gathering the weeds you root up the wheat along with them. Let both grow together until the harvest; and at harvest time I will tell the reapers, gather the weeds first and bind them in bundles to be burned; but gather the wheat into my barn" (Matthew 13:29).

It should be obvious that this is a parable about good and evil in society. Not in the individual. It is one thing to weed a small garden where there is room to work, and another to weed a large field where the plants are tightly spaced. Likewise, it is one thing to deal with evil in the individual soul and another to deal with it in society. Remember, this is a parable of the Kingdom of Heaven, the working out upon this earth of God's divine purpose for man's social existence. Jesus shared the dream of such a divine society which loomed so large in Hebrew history. His chief purpose was to revitalize that ancient hope and to prepare men who would be able to live in such a world. In explaining this parable later, he likened himself to the farmer sowing the good seed. Nowhere is Jesus' realism more evident than here. He is no idealist with his head in the clouds, assuming that because God wills it, the achievement of a divine society is a pushover.

Our world, and particularly the Church, is full of tired and cynical liberals who once labored under the illusion that a good society could be achieved by legislation and social planning and economic tinkering; that if you could get enough men of goodwill working together, all would be well. Alas, this has not proved to be the case. In our present society the hard-won achievements of civil rights are threatened, the laudable concern of society for the poor and aged is now, in reality, the welfare mess. A managed economy is being cursed by deficits and pockets of unemployment. Progress has resulted in urban sprawl, waste of natural resources, the pollution of air and water, and the arms race.

Jesus would understand all this. He's not surprised at weeds in the field of American society, threatening the American dream, and making cynics out of the dreamers. He knows the enemy never sleeps, never tires of trying to turn good into evil. He also would not be panicked into using drastic methods which threaten the vitality and the good, while destroying the evil, as many current proposals do. Too drastic remedies sometimes kill the patient. Don't trample down the wheat in uprooting the weeds. Be patient. Wait a while. And when harvest time comes, you will be able to save the wheat and burn the weeds. I would suggest that this parable is singularly pertinent to our own present situation. We need to be realistic, to recognize the vitality of that which is good in the American dream and not lose hope or become paralyzed by disillusionment.

And that brings us to the other two parables which are not stories at all, but simple analogies. One from the fields and the other from the kitchen. They are parables of hope, of small beginnings, and tremendous power. The Kingdom of Heaven will come, not in some spectacular display, but through the miracle of growth. A grain of mustard seed is but a tiny speck on one's finger, but dropped to earth, watered by the rain and warmed by the sun it becomes a plant strong enough for the birds to perch on its branches (Matthew 13:31).

Then Jesus turns to the miracle of bread, something that always fascinated me as a child. It began with an evening ritual in which Mother mixed a cake of yeast with flour, milk, and water, placed the small lump of dough in the bottom of a large pan at the back of the range, and the lump rose. The Kingdom of God is like that, says Jesus (Matthew 13:33). A holy fermentation at work, giving life to an inert mass of dough. It involves cooperation between man and God and a good purpose toward a good end. There are other kinds of fermentation at work in the dough of human society, and it's our job to let loose the power of God's spirit.

13

God's Decisions

THE story of the Prodigal Son is perhaps the most familiar of all the parables of Jesus. The New Testament rendering is so simple in its telling that on first thought it appears to need no interpretation. Yet, like all truly simple statements of the truth, it is so profound that each time one reads or hears it, some new dimension of its meaning leaps out of the familiar words.

It is called the parable of the Prodigal Son and so it is. It is centered on him, and yet the one who gives the story its deepest significance is the father. The primary reason for Jesus' telling it was to put in terms of a real and poignant life situation all that he meant by the love of the Father, God. But it also tells us much about man in his response to that love. It is all so elemental, so true to life, that it means as much today as it did when he first told it. In this story, one finds many themes woven together to make the whole. It is, for one, the classic expression of the conflicts and tensions between generations. It states the dilemma of the parent when confronted by the desire of a grown child to go his own way. It speaks of sibling rivalry between the good boy and the bad, the elder and the younger, and the different effects of inheritance and environment on members of a family. It is a story of the mystery and awesome danger of freedom and the results which ensue when it is misused. And it also speaks of the process by which man reverses his direction and seeks forgiveness and redemption from the love on which he has turned his back. These are a few of the themes to be found in this story, and over the years, I have used them all.

But another theme strikes me and that is the light this story throws upon the decisions and choices each of us has to make, the reasons for making them, their inevitable results, and how they affect our relationships to others.

The different choices of the two brothers were, of course, determined by their differences in temperament and personality, but the reason was the same for each—self-interest. We usually make choices for selfish reasons. The older brother conformed to the family pattern. He stayed home, worked hard, behaved himself, and gave his father no concern. We're not told what he thought when his brother hit the road, but his bitter reaction when the younger lad returned illuminates the record. He probably had it all figured out that with his rival gone, he was now secure. Any increase in the assets of his father's farm would be his someday and he could look forward to a comfortable future even though his father seemed to take him for granted. He had it made. His obedience would pay off.

The younger brother chose a different course, but for the same self-centered reasons. He wanted out. He felt he had no future at home; he was probably tired of having his older brother thrown at him as a good example. But more than this, with cocky self-assurance, he felt qualified to take on the world. The chief thought he gave to his father was to his father's bank account. He gambled on the old man loving him enough to give him his share and let him go. So the younger son made his decision. As someone once said, "temptation is the sneaking in of the immediate," and to this boy, *now* was the only thing that mattered. The future would take care of itself, so the heck with the long look and the careful stance. Let me live my own life and let me do it now. So, Dad, give me what I shall inherit someday, and let me go.

The father did just that. That was his choice, his decision. A lot of fathers would probably consider him a fool. He might have refused, given the boy a sound thrashing, put him under his discipline, and kept him home. It is interesting to conjecture what might have happened in that case. Certainly the boy would have been a reluctant worker and a constant problem. And just as certainly, the tension between the two brothers would have grown until the sad story of Cain and Abel might have been repeated.

In the father's difficult, and to us questionable choice, we must remember that Jesus is talking about God's choice when he gave man the privilege of choosing. The God of Judaism was not that kind of God, in the way that most men are not that kind of father. It seems easier and more natural to hold on, to rule and direct, discipline and punish, to try to coerce one's children, after they are grown, into the old ways of conformity. The God of the temple and of the scribes and Pharisees was that kind of God. Jesus' God was not. And in arriving at that conclusion, Jesus was a lot more realistic than we like to admit. Let us not think that the father was weak, or vacillating, or too easygoing. He faced an exceedingly hard choice which carries within it its own discipline. For one thing the father, once having made his decision, could do nothing but wait. He did not leave home to look for his boy when no word came. All he did was go to the gate every day and look down the road for the familiar figure which never appeared. He stood firm and waited because this was the self-limitation which his love had put upon him.

It is not otherwise with our Father, God. When the boy returned and his jealous brother resented all the fuss made over him, the father made it quite clear that all the estate would remain the elder brother's. The younger was restored to the family, but what he wasted was not restored. The story of the younger brother begins and ends with a division. When all his money was gone and he was reduced to the most despicable employment a young Jew could imagine, tending pigs, the record says he came to himself. He looked at the mess he had made out of his life. He faced his shattered ego

God's Decisions

and wasted life. The home he had once left in disgust, now seemed so good, and the thought crossed his mind that even the hired hands on his father's farm were better off than he.

This is still self-centered thinking, but with a tremendous difference. The cocky young man with the world by the tail was gone. He never really had existed. He was false, a phony. He thought he could make a go of it on the material things and the freedom his father had given him, but he found he needed more. He needed the love which he had spurned, the presence he had resented, the discipline against which he had rebelled. In seeing his real self and his real needs, he made another decision. To stand on his own feet, to get out of the stinking pigsty and to go home where he belonged. He would not ask to be restored as a son and heir; he knew he didn't deserve that. All he would ask was that he be given a job as a hired hand in the fields, working for his brother.

So he went home. He had a nice little speech rehearsed, which his father never let him finish. All we know is that the love which had waited so long was there to greet him with open arms and tears of joy. We do not know the end of the story. Did the elder brother get over his resentment and jealousy? Did the younger adjust to his new life? I dare believe the answer is "yes" to both these questions. But one thing is quite clear. The decision of God, as exemplified in the father in this story, is irrevocable. It is the decision to love enough both to let his son go and to receive him back again. It is a decision to grant him freedom.

But a man's decisions are not irrevocable. Sometimes pride or stubborness or just plain habit will confirm us in our own wrong decisions until our misused freedom plays itself out to the end. Yet once we see the consequences, recognize ourselves as we really are, we can revoke the original decision and make a new one which reverses the downward trend and turns our faces toward home.

14

God's Healing Power

THE healing of the Roman centurion's servant is one of the most dramatic of all the healings of our Lord. Its drama stems from two things. First, that the centurion was not a Jew, but a hated and despised soldier of Rome. And second, it was because the healing took place without Jesus seeing or touching the man who was sick of the palsy.

There are at least two things which make us wary of faith healing. First, there is no place where people can go overboard so completely as in this matter. In every healing movement that has sprung up within the Church, there is always the danger of fanaticism, of wishful thinking, and of denying the obvious benefits of medical science and surgical skill. The faith healers have many tragic cases of neglect to answer for where people have suffered needlessly and died prematurely. Less obvious to the lay person, but very real to the pastor, is the fear of this mysterious power which every minister knows is real, but which seems to be so unpredictable—now healing, and again failing to heal, and when there is a failure, leaving scars in the heart of the believer who seemingly has been passed by. As we turn to the gospel record of our Lord's healing ministry we begin to get some light on the problem and a clear indication of the truth.

First, our Lord himself seems to have had some of the same misgivings I have mentioned. There is no indication in anything he ever said or did that he believed healing was automatically and always God's response to man's faith and prayer. He was as concerned to help men triumph in spite of adversity as he was to remove adversity.

Secondly, there is no indication in the gospels that all the sick, all the deaf, dumb, and blind who crowded round him to be healed were healed. We may believe that for every leper cleansed there were hundreds who weren't. Nor is there any indication that it was because of lack of faith.

A third element in the gospels that has a direct bearing upon all this is the frank and realistic acceptance of the death of the body as the inevitable lot of everyone born into the world. The New Testament does not gloss over death and all the hard experiences that go along with it. Our Lord knew, and the New Testament writers knew, that our bodies were not meant to last forever, that they grow old and wear out, that they are subject to accidents and disease. But more than that, Jesus knew and the New Testament writers knew, that the ultimate death of the body was, for the Christian, not the last grim victory of nature, but relief and triumph for the spirit. That is the whole meaning of the cross and the empty tomb, and of Paul's great song of victory wherein he defies death to show its sting and the grave to claim its victory (1 Corinthians 15:55). Yet when we have said all this we have still not come to grips with the plain fact that God's healing power did then, and does now, show itself in amazing ways and would, I believe, show itself more often if it were not for some lack in us.

Going back to the story of the centurion and his sick servant, what do we find? In the first place it doesn't make a particle of difference to God who it is that needs and wants his healing power. Our Lord's response to the appeal of the Roman captain was as clear and spontaneous as that to any Jew. That the centurion was uncircumcised, a hated conquerer of God's people, a non-member of the synagogue, made no difference. It never does. And the reverse side of this is quite terrifying when you stop to think about it. There is no single instance of the healing of a Pharisee, a scribe, or a priest. Jairus, the ruler of a village synagogue, was the only religious leader I can think of who appealed to Jesus for healing when his little daughter lay sick unto death. Those who were healed were largely nobodies, outcasts, or foreigners. They were not the pious, the prosperous, and the rich.

Perhaps there is some relationship between this and the

fact that there is more indifference to and doubt of God's healing power among conventional proper church people than anywhere else. Is it because our faith is poured into too set a mold? Is it because we are afraid to let ourselves go in faith for fear we will be thought queer or naive or just plain zany? I don't know, but sometimes I wonder.

A second thing this story tells us is that a deep and profound faith is the absolute prerequisite for God's action. It need not be necessarily the faith of the one healed. Often it is the faith of someone else. It was the centurion's faith that led to the healing of his servant. There is no question in my mind how important faith is. More than once in my ministry I have seen a person come back from unconsciousness and extreme danger to normal health and strength. When the doctors had given up, it was a husband or a wife who believed as the centurion believed.

There is such a thing as God's healing power. It is a mysterious thing since it is of God, and is a dangerous thing when man misunderstands it or presumes to control it. It works, I believe, through the personality and the skill of every conscientious physician because medicine is of God, if anything is. But an increasing number of physicians are coming to see that there is much more to that power than what they possess and can use. It is that *plus,* that entrance into the sick body and mind of something far above all medicine, all surgery, and all therapy that could be ours more often than we know. That something can mean the difference between death and life, misery and contentment. That something is just as available today as it was when our Lord said to the centurion, "Go; be it done for you as you have believed" (Matthew 8:13).

15

Seek Ye the Lord

"SEEK ye the Lord while he may be found, call upon him when he is near" (Isaiah 55:6).

There is an old proverb which says it's never too late to mend. It is a comforting proverb and like all proverbs it has enough truth in it to endure. Just often enough one sees a complete change in the personality or direction of a human character to make one sure that this is so, yet most of us are very much like the youthful Augustine, who when driven by his passions, prayed to God to make him chaste, but not yet! Some day we mean to settle down, to root out our evil habits, to give God a chance at our vile tempers, but not just yet. Some day we are going to stop being selfish and give of our wealth and time to others. Some day we are going to find a real place for God in our busy lives. But not yet.

The tragic truth is that there are some important decisions in this life which cannot be put off indefinitely. Waiting to see what breaks is not an adequate solution to our problems for several reasons. For one, life is a process, a dynamic moving thing, which does not wait upon man's convenience or preference. For another, there is an innate logic to life. Every moment is the product of those which have gone before and holds within it the germ of the future. It is the logic of life that fixes habits and determines character. The law of habit is an iron law. Bend your being to some selfish pursuit, bind it to the amassing of wealth or the passion for power, and these things will have their way. Death in the bunker underneath the ruins of Berlin was the logical end of Hitler. Behind all the talk about fulfilling one's destiny is this logic; it is true of men, social orders, and nations. Call it the stars, call it fate, call it what you will, life does have this inexorable quality in it.

Yet if that were the final word, I shouldn't be preaching this sermon. Fate, destiny, and the logic of life are incomplete answers to man's questions. They leave too many important things unaccounted for. They leave out what happens when man turns to God. Of course this business of turning to God to break life's unyielding logic and to alter one's destiny is no easy matter. Those words, "seek" and "call" are decidedly imperative in mood. They are commands which can be obeyed only in action. One seldom happens upon God by accident. One must go after him. Hunt him out. Try and try to find him in every situation of life. The prize is not dropped into one's lap in answer to a passing wish. It is won at a cost.

How is God won and what does it cost? In the first place, God is the reward of the patient seeker. Judging by what I know of myself at least, patience is not one of our virtues. We want things to happen quickly. We have a passion for short cuts. It would be easier, and probably a lot more profitable, if knowledge of God could be guaranteed in fifteen or twenty simple lessons. But it can't, as anyone knows who has set out with that idea in mind. Nothing that is great can be won that easily. No skill in art, music, medicine, or religion comes that way, but rather by the slow, halting, patient, trying process which alone leads to the mastery.

Knowledge of God is won by the humble seeker. I am impressed by many characteristics which all the great research scientists of history seem to have in common, such as resourcefulness, courage, single-mindedness, and faith in arriving at ultimate goals. But more than all else, their great humility impresses me. Whether they were in the ordinary sense religious men or not does not alter the fact that in the presence of the great truths which they sought, they bowed as the creature to the creator. Not one of these men ever patted himself on the chest to exclaim, see what I have done! Always there seemed to be that certain quality in their characters which shrank from assuming their superiority over other mortals.

As one studies the lives of the great saints he comes again and again upon that same universal humility. Listen to St.

Paul. "I do not consider that I have made it on my own ... I press on" (Philippians 3:13). Or think of Jesus' reply to the man who addressed him as good master. "Why do you call me good? No one is good but God alone" (Luke 18:19). Yes, it is the ego in us which most often hinders our search for God. We might reach him if we could once get by our own selves. We might find him if we could lose ourselves, but this again is not easy and runs so counter to all our instincts. It does violence to the self-importance of natural man. Until and unless we can approach him as humble seekers and unprofitable servants, we shall not find him.

Finally God is found by those who seek him alertly. When one recalls how many go through the ordinary experiences of earth with eyes and ears closed and with unattentive faculties, it is not hard to discover why so many never find God. True, even the unobservant dullard usually awakens to some measure of awe and wonder before some unusual phenomenon of nature, and few men are totally unaware of God in certain important moments of life. But the alertness I am speaking of is something much more than mere awareness of the unusual, the striking, and the phenomenal. It means looking for God in the ordinary. There is an old saying attributed to Jesus, engraved on a Mohammedan mosque in India which goes like this: "Hew the wood and I am there, lift the stone, and I am there." In other words, look for God in the midst of drudgery and routine. Seek him in the low and the trivial. Think not that he is to be found only in crisis or in some rare great moment of illumination. These times come too seldom for any of us to rest our conviction of God's presence on them alone. It is not that there are only a few times and places and circumstances where he may be found, but a limitless number of them, if only we are alert enough to look for God in ordinary things and experiences, and to look for him *now*. We do not have to wait. And why should we wait when finding him would hallow each common task and make every bush aflame with God?

But alertness, like every other quality of the seeker, is a cumulative thing. The more we notice God in common things, the better are we capable of seeing him. I remember going through the long valley of a painful final sickness with a woman who told me this. She was not learned. Her secret was quite simple. All her life long she had made it her habit to look for God in pleasure and in pain, in bitter tragedy and in radiant happiness, in her home and in her social pleasures. She was constantly on the alert for some intimation of God. And the one concern of her last days of suffering was the fear lest she fail to get out of every moment an indication of the divine will and love.

I covet that secret for myself and for you. What a difference it makes if one approaches life with such a purpose. The things which without God are unbearable and incomprehensible, become through that quest for God, the evidences of his love and care. The amazing thing is that the seeker after him finally awakens to the fact that God himself is a seeker after us, and long before we begin to grope our way toward him, he has moved toward us. Seek him then in all patience, in all humility, and with all the alertness you possess. He is near now. Call upon him.

16

The Resurrection of the Dead

THE Easter festival, like so many high and holy days of the Christian calendar, is a curious mixture of many elements of our past. It is closely related to the Jewish Passover which falls at about the same time. It was at the Passover meal in the upper room where Jesus shared the lamb and salt and bitter herbs with his disciples, and broke the unleavened bread, and blessed the cup of Passover wine which forever after has had a special significance to Christians.

Yet the name we give to this festival is neither Jewish nor Christian, but pagan. Eástra was a northern European goddess of spring whose symbol was the egg. So when you send your children off on an Easter egg hunt, it is well to remember that this custom, though delightful, is an unconscious recognition in this sophisticated age, of an ancient goddess, otherwise forgotten except in the name of Easter day. But Christians do not crowd their churches to keep the Jewish Passover, nor yet to give a pleasantly sentimental nod

The Resurrection of the Dead

to a long-forgotten goddess of springtime. We come as Christians to celebrate an historical event whose importance eclipses all other events known to man: the resurrection of Jesus Christ.

The record of that event found in the four gospels is very simply told. The eyewitness accounts do not agree in all details any more than any four witnesses agree when recounting the same event. But the accounts do agree that when the disciples and the women came to the tomb, it was empty; their Lord was not there. Beginning with his enemies then, and continuing through the centuries, skeptics and scoffers have tried to break their stories down. No event in history has been scrutinized more critically, and no one has ever come up with any documented truth contrary to the gospel record. The understated, played down, simple record of the empty tomb and the gradual assurance of his followers that Jesus was alive forevermore is the reason we celebrate this day. We do not make of it a beautiful myth or a pious hoax, nor perpetrate a lie, but state a fact which cannot be successfully disproved. But this is not the only reason why Easter is the day of days for the Christian. If what happened in Joseph's garden is true, as we believe it is, then there is complete logic in our contention that Jesus Christ is still alive. It also makes sense, that since he lives in spite of the cross and the grave, so may we too if he is ours and we are his. This is the whole burden of the New Testament and it is still the great expectation of the Christian.

The Nicene Creed closes with a simple statement of that expectation—"We look for the resurrection of the dead, and the life of the world to come." We should understand right here that this change, this new existence, this survival which we look forward to after death is no easy hope held out indiscriminately to all men. There is a lot of loose thinking, even among Christians, about this hope, as though it were something an indulgent God held out to everyone willy-nilly. Nor is it a promise of universal immortality. In fact, the word, immortality, is used in only three places in the New Testament, and then only in contrast between that which is mortal or subject to death.

The great phrase of the New Testament is "eternal life." With the emphasis always upon *life*. Eternal life is a gift of God conditioned upon our response, and because we can never really earn it, it always remains a gift. To possess it, we must want it and accept the offer of it with our own free will. God does not force it upon us, as Jesus and the scriptures make so clear. That understanding always troubles me on Easter day. Is this gift so freely given that we think it can be assured by an annual gesture in God's direction? Do we consider God such an old softy that he can be impressed that easily? Or, if it isn't very important after all, why pretend it is on this day?

This "life of the world to come," this free gift the Father offers us, is something we have to want badly enough to look for it now. Jesus made it quite clear that eternal life is a state

The Resurrection of the Dead

of being which begins in this world. It is not something postponed to the next, nor can it be found unless we truly seek it. That is one meaning of that word, look. When you lose something of value, you look for it hard until you find it. When you know there is something precious worth having, you seek and seek. We seek fortune and success. We seek happiness and pleasure. We seek power and security. The scientist looks for new facts, the philosopher for new approaches to truth. But how hard are we looking for eternal life? Is it really something precious enough to seek after?

If it is, then it is something we can look forward to as well. That is another meaning of that word, look, which is not limited to our present search, but to our future expectation. Since what we are talking about is life, then that means the process of growth, and while as St. Paul says, it does not yet appear what we shall be, we know we shall be like Christ. This process begins any time a man sets his feet in the way of Christ and starts climbing. He learns as he travels. Some things he can only learn when the way is rough, others when it is beautiful, but all through the changing landscape of his earthly journey, he prays for the courage and skill to reach his goal.

The first time I drove north from California through the hot and dusty Sacramento Valley, I wondered if I should ever see a tree again or gulp a breath of cool air. But our goal was the Shasta country, and lured on by all we had heard of its beauty, we kept on through the almost unbearable heat. Almost imperceptibly, after we began to climb, the trees began to shade us, and though the canyons were stifling, every now and then a waft of coolness would engulf us, offering us intimations of what lay ahead. Then a storm broke over us with lightning, thunder, and rain. Winding and twisting on the old highway, stuck behind trucks and fighting traffic, we realized that it was cooler and the air was cleaner, and then without any warning, we rounded a curve and there was Mt. Shasta, towering into the blue, blue sky. I shall never forget seeing her for the first time. Nor the coolness of that night and the brilliance of the stars. Forgotten were the heat and the dust below. It was worth all the discomfort of that journey to be resting at Shasta's feet.

To me such a journey is a fair analogy to what I am trying to say. We had never been there, but others had, and we believed them when they said it was worth the journey. We were provided with maps which showed us how to go, maps which others had made. And having faith in our friends who had been there, and in those who charted the way, we reached our goal and found it beautiful beyond our imagining.

Somehow I must feel the same about the life of the world to come. I have been on that journey for quite a while and I know not how soon that curve will be rounded when, for the first time, I will glimpse the glory beyond all my expectations. But in the process of getting there, through heat and dust, storm and wind, starts and stops, and all the hazards and irritations on the way, I already possess a bit of what I hope someday to experience, just because I am looking forward in faith to reaching that high country. I've been moved to make this journey by all the saints in all the years who have charted the course, and even though I had no maps I would have to try it anyway, since Jesus has been there through death's gate and beckons me on through the centuries. I do look for "the resurrection of the dead, and the life of the world to come," and I urge you to join me in that great search and great hope without which life has no meaning and death is its only goal.

17

The Comfortable Gospel

BAD news is a curious thing. It crowds good news off the front page, it spreads faster, and it tends to give a distorted picture of reality. Somehow we seem to revel in bad news, rolling a morsel around on our tongues and spewing it out to anyone who will listen. We do not gossip about good things. We seldom spread good rumors. Rarely do we indulge in commendation, preferring rather to condemn. So the emphasis in our day is upon the depravity of men, the rebellion of youth, the inadequacy of our leaders, and the general decay of our culture. We talk about the weakness of the Church, the hypocrisy of its people, and its unwillingness to cut loose from old ways and live experimentally for Christ. No doubt all these things are true. The question is, are these things all the truth there is to see in our day?

No less than other men and other preachers can I overlook the bad news. I cannot be true to my calling and pretend that things are better than they are. Further, in the tradition

The Comfortable Gospel

which begins with the prophets, reaches its height in Jesus and the apostles, and continues to our own day, the message of doom and of judgment is an integral part of the teaching of the word. Nor does the role of the prophet confine itself to what are termed religious or spiritual matters. It is thoroughly secular, earthy and wide-ranging. Isaiah felt that God was vitally concerned in the foreign policy of his country. Amos saw God as one who demanded justice for the poor and outcast, and seeing it thus, condemned the wealthy and the law courts. Jesus agonized over the future of his race and religion and predicted the destruction of Jerusalem. He also attacked the greedy worldliness of the whole sacrificial system when he cleansed the temple on Palm Sunday. Paul was deeply concerned about the moral degeneracy of the sophisticated cosmopolitan cities of the Roman Empire. From the prophets of Israel on down through the centuries, doom and judgment and the frank recognition of the reality of bad news have been an integral part of the preacher's function.

But there is another side to this, easily forgotten in a chaotic and confused age. And that is that the gospel has to do with good news more than bad, with hope rather than doom, with redemption more than destruction. I suspect the time has come to recover this forgotten purpose which lies at the true heart of all that Jesus said and did. I would remind you that the word, gospel, means good news. Good news about God and about men. How desperately we need to hear that good news today, sounding with no uncertain tone the note of faith and hope and love amidst the noisy confused jangle of our times.

The sickness of modern man is due to loss of faith. He has little faith in anything, neither in government nor church nor law, nor in God, least of all in himself. There are credibility gaps everywhere, and until those gaps are closed man must flounder on toward anarchy and chaos. The root of this lost capacity for faith is essentially religious. And it is religion's business, above all else, to speak again the good news that man can believe, and that there is something he can believe in. For most people, God is dead. Even for too many church people. He has been lost in the stars, lost in the crowded streets, lost on the battlefields, lost even in the Church. Nor is it just a matter of finding the God of yesterday, if we could. That God *is* dead, whether we like it or not. Just as dead as the God trapped in the temple or locked up in a distant heaven was for the people to whom Jesus spoke and for whom he died. God meant as little to the run of men in Jesus' day as he does now.

But now, as then, the good news must begin as good news about the God of the present tense, not the one who was, but the one who is and will be. In this age of the impersonal, when man becomes a number fed into a machine, his thinking shaped by the mass media, his identity lost in the anonymous nature of life, the good news of a God who cares for the individual, who respects his dignity and work, who knows him by name and not by number, is no easy message to get across.

The Comfortable Gospel

Yet there is none more important, none more fundamental to the curing of the world's ills. For different reasons, it wasn't easy to convey this good news in Jesus' day. The little people who heard him gladly were pawns in the struggle for power. Neither those in the temple nor those in the palaces cared whether they lived or died, so long as their own selfish purposes were served.

Now, as then, this good news must be conveyed. Men must be given something worth believing in, greater than themselves. For interestingly enough, a man can't even believe in himself apart from a faith in a God who cares for him. I can't; neither can any of you. Why God cares, why he sees any value in my little life, is quite beyond my comprehension. But I believe he does. And without that faith I could not for a moment find any justification for my existence. You see, faith in God and faith in man are inseparable. Without the first, you cannot have the second. And without both, there is no hope. For hope is also a part of the good news so desperately needed in our day. And this hope, no less than the faith on which it is based, is solidly realistic and involves action on the part of those who do hope.

Jesus was under no illusion when he sat astride a donkey and entered Jerusalem amid the cheering crowds. He knew he was not the man on the white horse who would throw out the Romans and set up the Kingdom as his followers thought he would. Yet this very act was a symbol of his confidence in the long future, a measure of his hope which saw beyond the immediate situation in which he was involved and wherein he was doomed. It was an honest gesture; he did not pretend to be what he was not. He simply used what he had, was what he was, and accepted his friends for what they were, knowing that long after Rome collapsed and the temple lay in ruins, the future was his and belonged to those who loved him.

We need to remember all this in our own hope for the future and in what we do in our day. I am not a politician, nor an economist, nor a social worker, but I can contribute my hope that these can solve some of the problems of my day. I am just one citizen, just one little voice crying in the wilderness of concern for the future of America. But I can contribute my hope that God may yet use my country for the healing of the nations. But more than faith and hope, love is the basic good news we have to proclaim. This may, as St. Paul says, be the greatest of the three, and it certainly is the hardest to achieve and communicate. There is nothing soft about love at all. It too is realistic, unsentimental and difficult. Love makes demands upon us which we do not wish to accept. It breaks down barriers which we raise to protect us from those we do not like or of whom we are afraid. It disturbs our comfort and our ease.

Love is the good news which above all else communicates itself through action. One comes to faith most often because someone has demonstrated the fruit of faith in love. And I suspect that if the Church seems wanting in faith or hope to those who look at us from outside, it is because we do not love enough to care about sharing it with others. This then is the comfortable gospel we have to proclaim in deeds more than in words. But let's not misunderstand the meaning of that word, comfortable. It comes from the Latin, meaning to strengthen mightily. And when it is used in Bible or prayer book, that is exactly what it means. The good news is not something for us to sit back and enjoy in perilous ease; it is not for us, but for others that we learn its meaning.

18

Finding Life Right Here

"LOOKING for Life Out There," is the title of a cover story in an old issue of *Time* magazine. It was an exciting article based on the probes by American and Russian spacecraft cameras to discover whether there might be life evolving on the planet Mars. Mars did not cooperate too well, kicking up an unusually bad dust storm.

This article is a study in some depth of man's age-old fascination with the heavens. The mystery of the universe around us, with the orderly courses of the planets and the procession of the stars marking the changing seasons, holds the modern scientist in its spell, as it did his primitive ancestors. It is the nature of man, when confronted with a mystery, to attempt to unlock its secrets. He has an insatiable, and I believe, divine curiosity. For untold centuries he has looked at the heavens, and as he has become more and more aware of its awesome order and power, the heavens have been associated in his thinking with the ultimate creative force. Thus the scientist and the religious man, as they look up at the night sky, are both spellbound by the stars.

But that spell involves man in thinking about himself, what he is, why he is one of the many living creatures on this lesser planet of a lesser star we call the sun. The more he knows about the universe, the deeper he penetrates into its mystery, the more persistent and profound become his questions about himself in relation to that universe.

This is not a new quest. The pseudoscience of astrology sees a real connection between the stars and men. It so happens that I was born under the sign of Gemini, the twins. I am therefore a weird mixture of conflicting impulses, creative and lazy, idealistic and earthy, constant and fickle, hot and cold, generous and self-centered; a thoroughly screwed up person indeed. (I've often wondered if Peter were not a Gemini.) Yet even astrology offers hope for the likes of me, depending upon what planet is in the ascendance or what the sun, moon, and stars were doing at a given time. Frankly I do not need a horoscope to tell me I'm this kind of a person. I know it, my family knows it, my friends know it. In checking my references for the first part of this sermon, I asked a librarian friend to get me a good, easy layman's book on astrology. After looking at page after page of charts, symbols, and tables of ascendancy and conjunction, I decided that it was much simpler to go back to what I've known all along; that being human, original sin is a simple explanation of me, touched perhaps by the saving grace of Jesus my Lord.

So I go back to the psalmist who, looking out at the night sky, penned these familiar words: "When I consider your heavens the work of your fingers, the moon and the stars you have set in their courses, what is man that you should be mindful of him? the son of man that you should seek him out?" Then to hear the answer in his own awe-struck soul. "You have made him but little lower than the angels; you adorn him with glory and honor . . . " (Psalms 8:4). Or I think of Amos, the uncouth shepherd of Tekoah who, brooding about the injustices of his day and time, could cry out in the midst of his blistering attack on the leaders of church and state, challenging them to seek him "who made the Pleiades and Orion . . . whose name is the Lord" (Amos 5:8), and I find in these ancient insights a connection between the stars and man which is as valid now as it ever was.

But modern scientific man, obsessed with the mystery of life itself and learning more and more about the universe, is not content to assume that this one tiny speck of stardust is the only planet in thousands upon thousands of galaxies where life may be possible. Having solved the basic mysteries of the moon and finding it lifeless, he now begins to look farther afield in quest of life out there, somewhere in the infinity of space. And what is more, he may find it before some of you young ones are dead. This does not disturb me in the slightest, nor does it play havoc with my religious convictions. I have lived too long to make the egotistic assumption that this is an earth-centered universe, and that the likes of you and me are the only intelligent living things and therefore the favored darlings of creation. If, as I believe, God is infinite, then what he has done on earth he can do anywhere he wants to in this universe. And who knows, maybe he has received a lot more cooperation from his creatures elsewhere than he has here. I have no quarrel with looking for life out there.

Exciting though that prospect may be, the thing that seems to me far more important for us earthbound mortals is finding life right here. For no matter what our scientific explorations may reveal about the rest of the universe and its potential for life, you and I are creatures of earth. This is our home. This is where we have to work out our destiny. And we are a part of that human race which, for untold centuries, has tried to read in the stars, in one way or another, the meaning of life on this planet. Therefore, it is more than a little significant that Christmas comes in the year's darkest and stormiest days and that the whole story of Jesus' birth brings the heavens and the earth together in recounting that far-off divine event.

It was the shepherds on the hills, keeping watch over their flocks by night, to whom the angel appeared amidst the stars. They were afraid, as men still are, of such phenomena, but heaven's voice bid them not be afraid, because the most important thing occurring that night was the birth of a little boy in a stable. That simple, earthy, natural event had touched the strings of heaven's heart and the morning stars sang to proclaim that birth. Myth? Perhaps. Poetry? Maybe. I do not know nor do I care, because in that child born that night long ago, man for nearly twenty centuries has found the meaning of life here and now on this insignificant planet called earth.

The conclusion of that beautiful story again brings heaven and earth together as the three wise men journey across desert and mountain following a star. Some astronomers have claimed to identify that star as a comet which swung across the sky from east to west for some time before disappearing in the vastness of space. That is interesting conjecture, but again I do not care about its validity, because for the Magi the importance of the star lay in what it led them to in Bethlehem. To look for a king was their intent and to follow the star wherever it went. It was a strange kind of king they found. He was not in a palace. He was not in Jerusalem, but in a tiny little village nearby. He was not attended by courtiers but by the ox and the ass. He was to grow up at a carpenter's bench, take care of his mother and the younger children until he was thirty, then wander around Palestine as a peripatetic rabbi because no synagogue would have him. His popularity was short-lived, and at the end his closest friends turned coward when the establishment found him too dangerous to have around. He died at the hands of one of the greatest emperors of history, hanging like a common felon on a cross. He was buried in a borrowed tomb. Some king.

Ah yes, some king indeed. The star and the wise men were

right. Heaven joined earth in recognizing what so many still find it difficult to recognize, that Jesus, the Son of Man, born in a manger, born of a woman, is the real key to our existence and the proclaimer of our destiny on this earth. So I offer you this Jesus who has helped me to find life right here. Never in all my years has this meant more to me than now. The infinity and mystery of space do not hold the awe for me they once did. When this life is over, I know that I shall not be lost in the stars because the stars themselves are creatures of the same unfathomable being who for us and for our salvation, came down from heaven and was made man. Somehow this is all that matters. The showmanship, the trappings, the drama of the Christmas Eve service seem singularly unimportant and singularly incongruous to what really happened long ago. What is important is that all, wherever you are, may find life right here through Jesus Christ our Lord.

19

Dependence on God

ROGATION Sunday is one of the most interesting reminders in our prayer book of a long-gone age. It takes us back across the years to the English countryside where on the days between the fifth Sunday after Easter and Ascension Day, simple farmers gathered in their parish churches to ask God's blessing upon the crops they had planted. The ground had been prepared, the seed sown, and during that lull which comes between planting and harvest, they took time off to pray to him who sends sunshine and rain and makes the seed grow.

Nothing could indicate more pointedly how far both modern man and modern religion have come from their simple origins as the survival of these Rogation days in the church calendar. Of course the Christian religion is not the only place where that is true. Unless I am misinformed, I believe American democracy is finding it a bit difficult to solve the problems of the complex scientific, urban society on

Dependence on God

the basis of a constitution worked out by farmers for an agriculture economy of two hundred years ago. The plain fact is that the form or pattern which our thoughts take in religion, government, and economics is years behind the pattern of our life. We are still bound by the thought form of simpler times. Our thinking has not caught up with our experience.

As we face this problem insofar as it concerns our religion, it will do us little good to spend our time longing for the return of a day that is gone. For one thing, time doesn't turn backward except in the imaginations of those pathetic people who cannot face present reality. For another, the good old days were not quite so good as they are cracked up to be. Not for one moment would you go back to the age that moved in colorful procession to the blessing of the fields! In one way there is a great similarity between the age which produced the Rogation days and our own. That age felt as even do we at the mercy of something bigger than itself. For them, this bigger something was a God whose favor had to be curried lest his caprice bring on famine and pestilence. With us, this bigger something is known by many names, but God is not one of them. You know what sort of thing I mean; it accounts for the dread and suspicion, the fear and hatred which overlie our world like a dark cloud. We personify it in dictators and leaders of opposition groups, but whatever we call it, it bodes no good for mankind. Furthermore, it is our feeling that this unseen power cannot be propitiated by prayer. It is relentless and invincible. And in the face of impending trouble we lack the consolations of that faith which, whatever its faults, did enable those of an earlier age to endure with hope and face a grim world with confidence.

This confusing and fear-provoking situation is the inevitable result of pushing God more and more into the far corners of the universe. Not that modern man no longer believes there is God. He does. But as science has unfolded the laws of nature and discovered the immediate natural causes of more and more phenomena, the very name of God has gone out of use as the explanation of anything except in that antique phrase one finds in insurance policies. God is no longer for us the direct and immediate personal power who touches a man's life at every point from birth to the grave. If rank on rank of fluttering angels no longer obscure the deity upon a far off throne, then other things do. It is air and ocean currents which bring drought and flood, heat and cold. It is natural law, not providence, which determines our weal or woe. It is scientific agriculture, not prayer, which produces a good crop. It is supply and demand, in short the working economic law, which determines prosperity or adversity, and not the moral law. It is not God.

We are apt to laugh at the way in which the men of Jesus' time put a horde of angels between God and man. But the laugh is on us, I'm afraid, for in place of angels we have set up all sorts of secondary causes which impinge on human life. Those causes are impersonal and relentless, and God is, if

Dependence on God

anything, further removed from vital contact with us. This impasse cannot be broken through by any tour de force which disregards or denies the conclusions of science. Any recovery of a sense of God's presence in human life which has validity for our own times must recognize these conclusions. Certain things have come through science which are all to the good. The fickle and arbitrary deity of the Middle Ages who had to be coaxed and cajoled into a favorable attitude toward his subjects is, fortunately, a deity which is gone. We know more about how God acts in certain conditions than any previous age has known, and so far as the physical universe is concerned, we are less like children crying in the dark and more like grown men facing the light.

But it is right at the point of our increased knowledge of the nature of life that modern life breaks down. For one thing our knowledge is too complex. The genius of science is to rule out everything except the particular bit of reality with which it is at the moment concerned. But since most of us are not scientists, we are bombarded with an unending barrage of facts and theories and results which are terribly confusing. Science has made our world infinitely complex. There is no coordinating principle by which we can take these bits of reality and weave them into a unified whole. The old adage "where ignorance is bliss 'tis folly to be wise," is at best a half-truth, but it certainly is difficult and disturbing to be wise as our age is wise. It is as the answer to the modern's need for unity and simplification that religion has one of its greatest opportunities. What a chance to recover a sense of the dependability of a God whose strength never tires or fails. What a chance to discover in the midst of chaos an order and a purpose which transcend all and comprehend all. What an opportunity to find in the ancient Christian concept of God's fatherhood something which will fill the empty throne room of man's soul and restore to him a sense of the dignity and worth of human life. The Christian affirmations are fundamentally simple, and if modern man makes these affirmations, the difficulties of a complex world may indeed be overcome.

I want to say a word about something so obvious to us today, and that is the tragic gap between knowledge and the ability to act upon that knowledge. How often we have been told that we possess enough knowledge and intelligence to rid the world of war, provide plenty for everyone, and otherwise solve our major social problems. Why is it then that we seem to be unable to do these things? I wonder if the answer to that question is not fundamentally an answer which religion alone can give. I wonder if we are not reaping in the social realm what we have sown by neglect and indifference in the realm of religious faith. Why it is we do not know, but man always lacks the will necessary to action when he loses the conviction that above and beyond his temporal affairs there are eternal affairs. Our systems have value only insofar as they correspond to that eternal pattern and our earthly lives have significance only when they are in vital relationship with God the Father. Neither moral standards nor the structure of human society can stand up for long without reference to the eternal. In an address to the University of California some years ago, Dr. J. Robert Oppenheimer, the great atomic physicist, stated that fact as forcibly as any preacher could ever put it. He was talking about the awful shadow which the harnessing of atomic power had cast over the world. He spoke in rather pessimistic terms about our lack of capacity, thus far, to control it for the well-being of mankind. He made a strong plea that we resist the mood of bitter cynicism which reproaches reality. Our task, he said, is not to reproach reality, but to comprehend it, to push on behind the reality of the physical world to that of the spiritual from whence alone can come the power to use the physical for the well-being of this world. There is no doubt in this great scientist's mind about man's utter dependence upon God for the moral insight and spiritual strength needed to save him from disaster. In a way far deeper than when those simple peasants, on these days before Ascension time, begged God to master nature's forces, we moderns need his help. We do well, therefore, to think more deeply and earnestly of our dependence upon him who has made the universe which must be cooperated with constructively or we perish. Without that sense of dependence we are lost. With it man may yet be saved from the things which plague him.

20

The Triumph of the Son of Man

THE resurrection of Jesus from the grave has been looked upon for centuries as proof of his divinity. It is the empty tomb and the forty days of Eastertide during which he appears to his disciples and transforms the carpenter of Nazareth into the Son of God and the second person of the Holy Trinity, that form the base of the traditional theology of the resurrection.

Yet as the years go by, I wonder increasingly if this is the only meaning of the resurrection, or even the most important one. Is this what the brief gospel records are trying to tell us? Is this what St. Paul teaches and the New Testament proclaims? And is this one reason why Easter becomes a beautiful charade of faith which we re-enact annually with little relevance to our daily lives? Perhaps Jesus himself is greatly disturbed at what the traditional theology of the resurrection has done to separate him from the rest of mankind. The eternal appeal of Jesus from his birth through

The Triumph of the Son of Man

the cross to the grave is that he shares our human lot. His proudest title, and the only one he ever claimed for himself, was the Son of Man. To see the resurrection as a sudden and sharp change from manhood to Godhood is to strip him of our robe of flesh which he wore so proudly, and to strip us of our incentive to share in his risen and eternal manhood.

Let me make it quite clear that for me there is no question as to the fact of his resurrection. I accept that with no reservations, both because of the simple, unadorned, eye-witness flavor of the gospel account, and because the living Jesus is very real to me. I know he lives. His aliveness is fully authenticated by my experience. I need no other proof.

But this risen Lord who means so much to me, like the risen Christ of the gospels, makes himself known, not as a glorified deity, but as the man of Galilee. There is no record of his being surrounded by an aura of heavenly life as he appeared to his friends. The only reason they have difficulty recognizing him is because of their blindness induced by sorrow and doubt. But when they do, the testimony is unanimous that it is he whom they see. The familiar form and face, the same look in his eyes, the same sound of his voice. He still wears proudly the robes of man's flesh, now scarred by the nails and spear of the cross. He eats supper with his friends, he prepares breakfast over the fire on the shore of Galilee in order that the hungry fishermen may eat. He speaks tenderly to Mary Magdalene in the garden. He offers his wounds to Thomas to ease his doubt. He helps them face the future instead of the past. It took him forty days to convince them, but once convinced they went out into the world, captives of his spirit, to tell men that their true manhood could be realized through following him.

Later on, when the convert Paul roamed the empire, preached his sermons, and wrote his letters, it was this same basic theme which he proclaimed. In his matchless statement of the Christian hope of the resurrection, in 1 Corinthians 15 he puts it very clearly. He contrasts Adam and Christ, not as a man and a god, but as two men whose impact on other men is so different. The tragedy of Adam is that being created in the image and likeness of God, he broke the image through his willful disobedience and died, remembered ever after as a being with great potential who failed to live up to it. This is what happens to us when we follow Adam and ourselves forget the original purpose of God when he created us with that divine potential. But then another man by the name of Jesus enters the human scene. Living up to man's highest potential and picking up the broken pieces of the Godlike image which Adam destroyed, he restores it to original beauty and dignity. And what is more, restores that image in every one who is caught up by his spirit. This is what Paul means when he writes, "For as by a man came death, by a man has come also the resurrection of the dead. For as in Adam all men die, so also in Christ shall all be made alive" (1 Corinthians 15:21). No matter how extravagantly Paul writes about Jesus elsewhere, he never loses sight of the fact that it

The Triumph of the Son of Man

is Jesus, the Son of Man, who redeems other men because he *is* a man. And it is this conviction which makes Paul so concerned with the quality of human life among his converts. In their daily lives, he wants them to be men who, like Christ, demonstrate what manhood really means to those who, like Adam, have lost the image of God.

Can we not see then in what different light this puts the festival of Easter? We come to celebrate the resurrection of a man by the name of Jesus whom the cross could not kill nor the grave hold. We come to take new hope for our own humanity from one who demonstrated, as no other ever has, the tremendous capacity of man to triumph over every condition, both within himself and within the world in which he lives. Apart from this there is no significance whatsoever in our being here. It is to your manhood and mine that Easter speaks.

We live in a world of men, you and I. That world is lost in doubt, frustration, and fear, of which we share. Our human condition is not good. In spite of his achievement, man's image is tarnished. But it is to just that sort of world Jesus came as a man of Galilee, and in such a world that the living Jesus in the lives of other men began the saga of our faith which is now nearly two thousand years in telling. Again and again over the centuries his gospel has had tough going. Sometimes the good news has sounded like bad news to the lost sons of Adam who have tried every means to suppress it, but never succeeded. It has had tough going in the Church from the very beginning as the New Testatment clearly states, because half-converted followers have not dared to walk with his confidence nor to demonstrate his love.

But the living Son of Man is as indomitable and persistent now as he has always been. His survival value is limitless. He cannot be stopped, because now here and now there, he takes hold of the unlikely stuff of mortal men like us and sends us forth once more into a lost world to live his life wherever we are and whatever the conditions we face. Do you believe that? If you profess to be a Christian and don't, then why are you here acting as though you did? Would you like to believe that? Then I say, quit worrying about how and whether he be God and accept him as the Son of Man who is ready to take your humanness and help you wear your own robe of flesh proudly in something of the original Godlikeness which Adam lost.

That kind of faith has tremendous pertinence to the tragedy of our times. The world awaits the appearance of men who have been with Jesus. Our talented and sophisticated generation will never believe through argument. It's only when they see another man in whom the Christ lives that they can begin to believe in God again. For you see, the distinction between the human and divine disappears in a man like Jesus. The Son of Man is the Son of God in the very quality of being a man at something like his best. To be truly manlike is to be Godlike as well. And the nearer one comes to being a man of Jesus' stature the closer he gets to knowing the glorious liberty of the sons of God. It is to such an experience you and I are called on Easter morning. This is our destiny and this is our hope.

THREE

For you were called to freedom . . . but through love be servants of one another.
Galatians 5:13

21

Words

WORDS are wonderful things. They are the symbols by which we convey to each other the product and richness of our experience. They are the materials out of which great poetry, great drama, and great preaching are built. They are the medium of conversation and social intercourse, they are among the most priceless assets of humankind. Words may be beautiful in expressing sublime thought and lofty inspiration. By them soul catches fire from soul, mind from mind. And they are useful too, for civilization is the product of man's experience preserved from age to age, and without words such progressive experience, such sharing of thought and feeling would be impossible.

As are all precious assets, words are dangerous. The very thing that makes for their beauty and usefulness can become ugly and harmful. Words can curse as well as bless, destroy as well as build. That is why I never climb into the pulpit without breathing the old psalmist's prayer, "Let the words of my mouth and the meditation of my heart be acceptable in thy sight, O Lord, my rock and my redeemer" (Psalms 19:14). Any man who will assay to preach learns the value and importance of words. They are the swift arrows which wing their way to the minds and hearts of his hearers. Sometimes those arrows must wound, more often bless, but the preacher dare not forget the power of words. This prayer of the psalmist is one we might well pray at the beginning of each day before we begin life with our fellows. Unfortunately, most of us are not aware of the divine love which broods over our every thought and word. But that awareness, that sense of God in our lives, gives us the essence of real religion. And I know of no better place for us to begin to feel his presence than to approach the business of speaking and thinking as in his sight.

The psalmist is right when he links the words of his mouth with the meditation of his heart, for words are expressions of thought. If our thoughts are wrong, they are bound to find expressions in wrong words. Worse yet is the absence of thought which produces the nonsense of so much of our conversation. By no stretch of the imagination can most of us lay claim to acceptability in God's sight of either our thoughts or our words. Someone has said that the fine art of conversation has fallen in our day before the babble of intelligent morons who know all the words, but lack any capacity for thought behind the words. Whether that is true or not is not for me to say. But this much is true, we are living in an age when the precious gift of language is wasted on the expression of many things not worth expressing. Our printing presses, the radio, and the hard cynical repartee of the sophisticated spew forth words in a steady torrent, much of which is sheer waste. We are a wordy generation and yet so much of what we have to say is not worth saying.

No one realized the need for economy in speech more than Jesus. The master used words as no other religious genius has ever done. He appreciated their value. He employed them to enlighten and inspire his hearers. For him words were too precious to waste. Simple, direct, forceful, he has left us sentences that are as sparkling and clear-cut as diamonds. His philosophy of words is clearly summed up in his discussion of swearing. "But I say to you, do not swear at all, either by heaven . . . or by earth . . . or by Jerusalem . . . and do not swear by your head, for you cannot make one hair white or black. Let what you say be simply 'yes' or 'no,' anything more than this comes from evil" (Matthew 5:34).

We need to go a step further in our study of this text. Not only do we say many useless and senseless things, but alas, many positively harmful things. St. Paul begins his matchless chapter on love with these words, "If I speak in the tongues of men and of angels, but have not love, I am a noisy gong or a clanging cymbal" (1 Corinthians 13:1). Would that those words could be emblazoned in every home, in the market, on the street, in our places of business and recreation. For nowhere is the uncharitableness of Christians more subtly apparent than in their speech. How often an otherwise stimulating conversation will descend to the depths of vulgar gossip. Without meaning to be malicious we have sat in judgment on our fellows because of our natural interest in other persons.

There is no place for gossip in a Christian society. A gossiping Christian is a contradiction in terms. Of course, we are interested in each other, we share our mutual woes, our mutual burdens bear. That is quite a different matter from the careless way in which we criticize each other. We do it in our homes where a child's innocence is poisoned by our judgments. We do it in our social life where eager ears are quick to catch some juicy bit which blights a reputation and mars a character. And even worse than gossip is innuendo. More harm is done by the merest suggestion of wrongdoing on the part of another than by positive open accusation. The trouble with this sort of unguarded word is that it plants the seed of distrust in the mind of the hearer. By the slightest suggestion of dishonesty or wrong conduct, we can blight friendships and destroy the confidence which is the basis of human relationships. The tragedy of thoughtless or harmful words is our inability to take them back. Once said, they go on their wounding way and no amount of correction on our part can affect the evil we have done. One of the most distressing aspects of our time is the ease with which we can sin in this regard. When nerves are on edge with the heightened pressure of our lives, it is so easy to speak a word in heat which can never be retracted. When people live in an atmosphere of tension and anxiety, it is so easy to become suspicious of others and to express that suspicion in the casual word which questions one's loyalty or blights a reputation.

Perhaps most tragic of all in its long-range effect is the universal use of words in times like these as weapons of hatred and ill will between nations, races, and creeds. And I wonder sometimes if some of the words spoken by our leaders may not someday come back like boomerangs. The words of our mouths must be acceptable in God's sight or they will be used by the devil. Unless we, like the psalmist, can set a guard before our lips through prayer and thought, we are in great danger indeed of harming both God, our fellows, and ourselves.

22

Patience

Count yourselves supremely happy, in the knowledge that such testing of your faith breeds fortitude, and if you give fortitude full play you will go on to complete a balanced character that will fall short in nothing" (James 1:3).

In St. Luke's church in San Francisco, we had seven beautiful sanctuary lamps hanging from a roof beam above the chancel rail. One Sunday morning three girls stopped to ask me what those lamps meant. Since we did not then reserve the sacrament which is the usual significance of such lamps, I had to think of something. I told them about the seven lamps which symbolized the seven spirits round about the throne of God in the book of Revelation. Quite obviously that meant nothing at all to their young minds, so I promised them that I soon would tell the whole Sunday school what those lamps meant. When a parson promises something to a child he has to deliver. So after racking my brain, I thought of seven spiritual gifts of Christian life and

Patience

named each lamp after one. Love, joy, peace, patience, kindness, neatness, temperance, were what I chose.

I can assure you that it was no intention on my part to have patience in the center of those seven lamps. But there it was ever afterward. Patience, hanging just a bit higher than the three on either side. Patience, right smack in the middle. Ironic indeed, that I of all people, would unconsciously put patience in that place of honor. And equally ironic that the tiny electric bulb in the patience lamp seemed to last longer than any of the others. Often a youngster would come up and say, love is burned out, or temperance is burned, or peace, or one of the others. But patience always managed to burn through a Sunday and then quietly expire during the week.

The longer I live and try to be a Christian, the more convinced I am that patience is the key to all these other virtues and that it is also the most difficult and the most God-like. Without infinite patience, God could not love the likes of you and me. Without patience, God could not hold persistent to his purpose in the crazy world of men. Without patience, he must have given up long ago and consigned us to the damnable state man seems so prone to seek. Likewise, it is our own want of patience that makes us intemperate, quarrelsome, unkind, wanting in love, and miserably unhappy so much of the time. Hard it must be for God, hard indeed, to be patient with us.

There are some people who are born patient, but not too many. The Christian's patience is sorely tried because of the very fact that he has set for himself a high standard of faith and conduct which is hard to attain. Without so hard a goal, one could afford to be patient because the demands upon him would be more equal to his inadequate powers. But when the standards are so high, the effort to reach them becomes so intense that we lose patience in the struggle. As a result there is no impatience equal to that of the thwarted idealist or the eager Christian who tries too hard.

For one thing he loses patience with himself. I don't know about you, but as for myself, my patience with others is in direct proportion to my patience with myself. Not a little of the petulance I show to others roots in a deep inner dissatisfaction with myself. I believe this is particularly true of anyone who would sincerely try to live the Christian life. We have set before us the highest possible standards of faith and conduct, and we fail ever and again to achieve those standards. We are told to love, and we find ourselves too preoccupied or maybe just too squeamish to put ourselves out for some unattractive, helpless, hopeless person. Then when we read about our Lord touching the loathsome, a wave of impatience sweeps over us at the inadequacy of our love. Or maybe there is some sin or weakness we want to get rid of. We try, honestly and sincerely for a while, and then that old evil thing crops up again the moment we ease up on the effort. And in our impatience we call ourselves spineless, or emotionally immature, or poor Christians, or just plain hypocrites.

Patience

It is at this point that we tend to lose patience with our fellows who move too slowly, get stuck on unimportant details, or throw up roadblocks of doubt and opposition in our way. Others, too, stumble and rise again only to fall once more. They seem to be blind and stupid as to the real purpose of living, and their ideals and standards fall short of what we think they ought to be. In other words, they are acting quite normal according to our own experience with ourselves. But because of our well-known ability to see the shortcomings of others better than our own, we get into a tizzy about the way other people add to our difficulties in living the Christian life.

And it is then that we are apt to get out of patience with God. We look at our own inadequate efforts, made more difficult by the inadequacies of others, and wonder why in the world God doesn't do something more about it. Why doesn't he take them by the scruff of the neck and make them what I think they ought to be? Why doesn't he take me? If his power is so great, why does he let this world fall prey to evil men and evil ideas which thwart his Kingdom and make it so hard to live as Christians. And out of that impatience, comes the Christian who stops praying or the parson who gets cynical, or the idealist who abandons his dreams, or the ardent fanatic who takes things into his own hands and starts playing God with his fellow men.

The plain fact is that we want to reach heaven by a single bound, to find quickly attainable goals for our striving, to have done with this business of falling and rising and falling all over again. But life for the Christian is not that easy. There are no short cuts to heaven, no easy road to self-realization, no sudden victory over sin.

We see this all too clearly in the life of Jesus. How patient he is with the people who throng around to be helped and healed. How long-suffering he is with the stupidity of the simple men who are his closest friends and disciples. When his enemies sought to trap him by their questions, he calmly asked them a few in return. When they confronted him with hard decisions, such as that presented by the woman taken in adultery, he held his temper by writing with his finger in the dust at their feet. When the chief priests mocked him and the soldiers spat on him and pushed the thorn-crown into his brow, he never said a word. When Pilate compromised and Peter lied and slunk away, he held his peace. When they nailed him to the cross, he did not rail at them in anger.

Patience—great God, where has man ever seen any like his? When has man's ever been tried as his was tried? How trivial our trials compared to his! His patience is the patience of God. His patience is the inevitable corollary to God's love. It is, if you will, the sign of his self-limitation. He prefers men to love him, but the necessary environment of love is freedom not to love. Love, to be real, must be a free response. That is why God doesn't push us around, make us be good, treat us like puppets on a string. He can afford to wait as love always must afford to wait. It is the realization of the patience of the heart of God, as revealed in Jesus Christ, that gives us patience. If our love is great enough, we too can afford to wait. It is a slow, unending, patient process by which we climb, and the goal at the end of the road is reached at long last only by those, who in the trial of their faith, have persevered in patience to the end.

23

Contentment

THE great secrets of Christian living are not come by easily. Usually they do not spring forth from some isolated moment of inspiration, but rather out of painful struggle. One of the things that endears the apostle Paul to so many is his constant repetition of this fact. His grasp of the significance of Christ's saving power was not gained all at once in the blinding vision which converted him. His early letters have a lot of the old Saul of Tarsus in them. The fanaticism, the self-assertion, the defensive attitude of the Pharisee, the natural fighter in him still predominate. He has much to learn of tolerance and charitableness and the sweet reasonableness of Jesus. He does not take opposition easily, nor take kindly to the criticisms of his enemies.

But the aging Paul in a Roman prison has come a long way on the road from those strenuous early days. He has learned much about the secret of Christ-likeness through the hard school of his own experience. That school included not

Contentment

only the successful planting of strong churches in Europe with all the thrill of empire-building, but it had also included imprisonments and beatings, stonings, shipwreck in stormy seas, and hollering mobs crying for his blood. It included battles with his own health and his enemies, the cold disdain of the Greeks, and quarrels with his friends. And then, at last, the bitter pill of finding his proud possession of Roman citizenship no guarantee against imprisonment and death. Yet out of the successes and failures of a stormy life he came at last to the place where, though in prison and facing death, he could write those sublime words to the Philippians, "I have learned to find resources in myself whatever my circumstances. I know what it is to be brought low, and I know what it is to have plenty. I have been very thoroughly initiated into the human lot with all its ups and downs—fullness and hunger, plenty and want. I have strength for anything through him who gives me power" (Philippians 4:11).

There is no boasting in those words, only the statement of a great fact, dearly learned. Nor is there any of that refusal to admit the reality of the difficult and unpleasant which is characteristic of certain kinds of modern religions. Abasement and exaltation, fullness and emptiness, plenty and want are all caught up together in the secret he has learned. The point is, he had to *learn* that secret just as most of us do. Few of us come to it naturally. And none of us can come by it without experience.

Take the experiences of want, emptiness, and hunger. Think of them first on the physical level which the apostle certainly must have had in mind. Sometimes those of us who have always had more than enough food, clothing, and shelter get a bit impatient with those who haven't. Impatient with their whining and begging, and more impatient still, with the bitterness and belligerence of those who have not towards those who have. It is easy enough to quote St. Paul to them, advising them to be content with whatever state they are in, but it takes a tremendous amount of grace to accomplish that difficult feat, and a lot more grace, I'm afraid, than many of us would have were we to change places with them.

But that interpretation of the apostle's words is really a travesty on what he means. Being content in spite of your lot is vastly different from being satisfied with your lot, and it is the first St. Paul is talking about when he wrote these words from a Roman prison. Being still a good fighter, he was trying to get out of his chains in order to be free again to preach the good news of Jesus. He would never be satisfied as a prisoner, but the chains could not stifle his spirit. He could still pray and sing and rejoice in the Lord. And that's finding contentment, even in his bonds.

The secret of such contentment is based upon at least two things. First, there is the necessity of learning that content or discontent are not so much a matter of the conditions of our physical existence as they are a matter of our inner spirit.

Contentment

It is perfectly obvious to any of us that this is so when we remember that contentment is not always found in the midst of luxury, and very often is found in the midst of poverty. In spite of the monstrous lie which we are fed so constantly by the advertisers, the good and happy life does not depend upon the satisfaction of our material needs. Something of that lie has spread to our dreams of a future society in which freedom from material want shall guarantee peace to the world.

From the standpoint of the Christian gospel that is not only heresy but blind and unrealistic thinking. True, a man needs certain things to satisfy his physical life, and our Lord was one of the first to recognize those needs. Health is better than sickness, plenty is better than want, cleanliness is better than filth, and freedom better than slavery. Better, not only for the physical man, but for the spiritual man as well. But when we have recognized all this we still have not gotten at the deeper needs of man's spirit. The need to be loved and to love is greater than the need for food. The need to be understood is greater than the need for shelter. The need for a great, all-consuming purpose is greater than the need of help. We are told that St. Paul was a sick man all his life. His eyesight was so poor that he had to use a secretary to write his letters, and there is also the probability that he suffered from epilepsy. But no man in perfect health could exceed the strenuousness and skill of his crowded ministry. Captive of a great purpose, he was enabled to override his infirmities, even to use them as assets rather than as liabilities.

I remember the captain of the great liner upon which I returned from Europe many years ago. We were invited to the captain's tea one afternoon, but the captain was not there. The chief steward explained that the captain was having his customary bout with seasickness. Having just gotten over that awful malady myself, it passed my comprehension how any man could be a sea captain on those terms. But you see, he loved the sea and he loved his ships, and captive to the purpose of his life, even his infirmities were ignored. Yes, contentment does depend upon the spiritual life of man. And unless love, purpose, and joy and peace are the proud possessions of our souls, we shall never be content no matter what the external environment may be.

But even this is not all the secret. For St. Paul, as for every real follower of Christ, there is another thing which gives contentment a peculiar Christian quality, and that is dependence upon the strength that is within Christ. "I have strength for anything through him that gives me power" (Philippians 4:13), cries the apostle after he has testified to his acquired ability to abound and be abased. In other words, this ability is not of his own making, nor solely the product of experience. It is God-given. It is the result of nothing quite so much as constant contact with the living Lord. When one remembers what manner of man Paul was by nature, it is easier to believe that. He was impatient, imperious, opinionated and fanatical, and of all personalities in the world, that sort has the least natural chance of learning how to be content. But when such a man stops trying to force life to his own pattern and seeks only to follow Christ's pattern, the secret can be learned. The tremendous drive and strong will is redirected by a great love and a great purpose not one's own. Good fortune or ill fortune, success or failure, plenty or want are taken in stride by those who seek above all else to do Christ's will. For contentment in its truest sense is a by-product of the lifelong effort of a man to walk with Jesus.

24

With a Quiet Mind

IF MODERN man could be said to want any one thing more than all others, that thing is peace. Peace in the world and peace in his own heart. There is always a vital connection between the inner and outer quality of men's lives. Discord in society is always the expression of souls not at peace within themselves. And social discord in turn makes the acquirement of inner peace much more difficult. There is nothing new about this observation. The collects of the church year reflect this yearning for peace in other times. Take for example, the collect wherein we pray that "this world may be so peaceably ordered by thy governance, that thy Church may joyfully serve thee in all godly quietness" (Collect: fifth Sunday after Trinity, *The Book of Common Prayer*, 1928). This is obviously the cry of a desperate man looking out on the world's chaos for which there seems to be no human cure, and longing for the church to be free from the pressure of a hostile world so that it can enjoy God in peace and tranquility. I can have some sympathy for this unknown Christian as I wish at times all problems could be solved with ease. But, alas, this is not the case, and I'm not at all sure we should like it if it were. There is, however, another collect for the twenty-first Sunday after Trinity (*The Book of Common Prayer*, 1928), which digs deeper into the quest for peace. "Grant, we beseech thee, merciful Lord, to thy faithful people pardon and peace, that they may be cleansed from all their sins, and serve thee with a quiet mind."

Just when this prayer was first uttered, we do not know, but it is probable that it originated in one of those bitter crises when the Roman Empire was collapsing and all the world was in chaos. Certainly one could not pray such a prayer with all its deep insight and feeling in any moment of relative quiet and contentment in the affairs of men. Such longing for peace and a quiet mind could only come out of the midst of strife and confusion. There is a forthrightness and simplicity about it which could be born only out of a real need. Let us admit at the start that a quiet mind is not easily come by for most of us. The distractions of the busy world, the worries and anxieties over loved ones, the concerns of business and day-to-day life see to that. These things crowd in upon us so incessantly that most of us have few moments of freedom to order our thinking and to view life objectively. It becomes even more difficult to persevere, let alone find serenity, when we move out of these private concerns into the noisy confusion of our age. In the very moments of preparation for this sermon, my ears are assailed by a weird jumble of dissonant sounds made by passing cars, the screech of brakes, the wail of sirens, and all the other noises which are part of life in a big city. Even the thick walls of God's house can't keep them out. And when we add to the roar of man's machines the roar of angry partisan voices, both near and far, dominating every phase of our common life, there is almost a sardonic humor in even hoping for a quiet mind.

Yet it is just now, in a time like this, that we need it most. You need it and I need it; desperately, urgently, if the Babel which is our world is not to drown out the whispering of the still small voice within our souls, and the soul of humanity. The attainment of a quiet mind is both an achievement and a gift. It involves certain things we must do before God can give us what we need and seek. So let us look first at our part in that attainment.

There are at least two things upon which God's gift of a quiet mind is conditioned. First, it implies faithfulness. "Grant . . . to thy faithful people," is the way this ancient prayer puts it, which seems to indicate that one who lacks the capacity or willingness to have adequate faith in God has little hope of achieving inner repose. For faithfulness roots in the conviction that there is a God, that he cares for his children, that he wills us to live courageously and victoriously and to trust him in whose hands are the issues of our lives and the life of mankind. To develop and hold a conviction like that is very hard in a time like this. It is hard enough for us. How much harder it must be for millions of our fellows who are desperate, starving, and homeless. We are indeed pious fools if we think otherwise. Yet we should be worse fools if we forget that that very conviction was born out of the agony of the cross and nourished by the blood of the martyrs. It is too great a conviction and too important to us to be had cheaply. The pearl of great price is not to be had for a dime.

So great and comforting a faith is born paradoxically enough out of man's tragedy. The deeper and more profound the tragedy, the higher and more profound the faith that overcomes it. And if our world is to be saved, no cheap little faith will do it. It is the expensive kind, the kind that costs so much that it hurts, that will perform that new miracle. So let us not seek peace of mind at the bargain counter where we think a little faith will suffice. No wonder so many of us don't find it or find only what passes for it, and discover too soon that it is shoddy and won't wear well. Think not that repeating the creed or reciting the Lord's prayer or coming to communion when it is convenient or attending church fairly regularly is all there is to it. It is all these and more, much more. It is remembering you are God's child at work and at play. It is remembering that your privilege of being his child is the privilege of every living soul who will claim it. It is refusal to be swept from that recollection by personal tragedy or social pressure. It is hoping against hope, trusting when all the evidence tells you you are wrong. It is seeing the cross as a sign of victory in the midst of defeat and heaven in the midst of hell. It is, in short, being so faithful that in the paraphrase of Paul's great words, neither life nor death nor present danger nor future fear nor anything else will be able to separate you from the love of God which is in Christ Jesus, our Lord (Romans 8:39).

The other thing implied in the collect which we must do to obtain the quiet mind is repent. When we ask of God to grant us pardon that we may be cleansed from all our sins, it is ridiculous for us to suppose that we can get that without repentance. There is nothing whatsoever in the gospel which indicates that pardon and cleansing from the stain of sin comes any cheaper than faith comes. I wonder sometimes if the present disquietude of man is due half so much to his lack of faith as to his unwillingness to repent. You know as fully as do I from first-hand experience that a quiet mind and unrepented sin cannot exist in the same personality. And if that is true of the individual, why should it not be true of men en masse? If the guilty conscience of a murderer can drive him mad, is it so strange that the collective sin of mass murder which is war and for which no single nation, neither victor nor vanquished, has ever repented, should produce the madness of this century? Unrepented sin produces that inner discord which leads inevitably to further sin.

But repentance involves the humiliating experience of

being stripped of our robe of pride and seeing ourselves as we really are. It involves admitting to God always, and sometimes to other men (which seems to be harder yet) that we are miserable sinners, that we have indeed fallen short of our high calling, have missed the mark, and have lost our way. And it means more positively an about-face, a complete reversal of goals, so that God's will, not ours, becomes the main objective of our lives. Faith and repentance dearly won at real costs are the absolute requirements if we are to know the quiet mind.

And what of God's gifts: pardon, peace, and cleansing? Yes, it is when we begin to experience these things which he does for us that we realize how little we have done after all. And somehow through the miracle of his grace, the peace of God grows and grows with each fresh experience of his love, until at length we know the glory of a mind made quiet. Not through some transitory drug, nor yet through turning our backs on reality, but through faith in him under whose banner the eternal victory shall be won. Like the child who, weary of the day, all soiled and dirty, plunges into his bath and is tucked in all clean and safe and warm, holds his mother's hand and begs forgiveness for little wrongs, and waits in certain expectation of her goodnight kiss. So we, grown old and soiled by bigger wrongs, can know the thrill of cleansing and can grasp with equal confidence the loving hand of God.

25

Kindness

The quality of mercy is as uniquely Christian as any I know and for that reason it is about as hard as any to achieve. No less a person than Plato had serious misgivings about mercy. That was why he gave such great encouragement to the Greek tragedies on the assumption that the people watching the actions on the stage could get pity and kindness out of their systems in a relatively harmless way. Even the Old Testament seems to have some question about mercy. It was not until the preaching of the great prophets, such as Isaiah and Hosea, that the mercy of God began to overshadow his justice, and the old law of an eye for an eye and a tooth for a tooth was brought into question as a potential travesty on the character of God.

If one may judge our own century by the evidence, it would seem to have forgotten too often that mercy is a virtue. Seldom has the individual counted for less or his life been held more cheaply. We have seen so much brutality, so much

Kindness

human woe and suffering, that a creeping callousness has invaded the spirit of man in our day. There is no mercy in the machines we have created, no mercy in modern warfare. Therefore the plea of Christ, "Be merciful, even as your Father is merciful" (Luke 6:36), seems to go unheeded. Jesus then goes on with simple and yet terrifying realism to show how mercy, or the lack of it, works itself out in human life. He states that without it one cannot escape the charge of desperate hypocrisy. The modern versions of the Bible give us an important clue to the nature of mercy. The mercy of God is called loving kindness, and human mercy is called kindness more often than not. So what we are really thinking about is the nature and the results of kindness.

On first thought, kindness would seem to be quite a common virtue easily taken for granted. Yet few of us are as kind as we think we are. And Shakespeare to the contrary, the quality of mercy is too often strained and does not drop as the gentle rain from heaven upon the place beneath. For too many of us mercy is not the persistent habit of each day, but something which is squeezed out of us in moments of crisis when the unconscious thoughtlessness and subtle cruelty of ordinary behavior disappears temporarily for urgent reasons. Yes, there is more to mercy than most of us dream, for the loving kindness of Christ is far above that which is purely natural.

What then is the mercy, the kindness, the compassion about which our Lord is talking? For one thing, mercy is

Christian love in action—persistently, habitually, and wholeheartedly. Like all other Christian qualities it results from man's response to the mercy he has seen in God. The loving kindness of God is the most unique thing in the Bible's conception of God's character. "But thou, O Lord, art a God merciful and gracious, slow to anger and abounding in steadfast love" (Psalms 86:15). "As a father pities his children, so the Lord pities those who fear him" (Psalms 103:13). "Surely his goodness and mercy shall follow me all the days of my life" (Psalms 23:6). These are only a few of the great Old Testament statements about the loving kindness of God. Then, all of God's kindness, which man had but glimpsed before, became a living reality in the kindness of Jesus. His brief ministry was in itself one great act of mercy. To the sick, the stupid, the sinful, and the outcast, he brought a heart full of compassion and tenderness which showed man not only the infinite loving kindness of God, but what man's kindness really could be when touched by the hand of God. Small wonder then that his followers have laid upon us the compulsion to be kind.

A merciful Christian is first of all a tender-hearted and compassionate man. Using modern terms we might say that kindness involves a high sensitivity to the moods and the needs of others. Few of us are born with that sensitivity, but all of us can acquire it if we will. Tender-heartedness roots in the unself-centered nature of real love. One who looks at life as something of which he himself is the center, can never be kind as Christ was kind. If my needs, my moods, and my desires are the most important thing to me, than I will not be kind because I cannot be on that self-centered basis. The sensitive man is often a cruel man. Going through life in his egocentric way he carries a chip on his shoulder and often strikes out at others before they get a chance to strike at him. Such a person can become the essence of kindness if God gets a chance at him. His very ability to be hurt can be turned about so that he is more keenly aware of others' hurts. His tendency to strike out at life can make him better able to see why others strike out, and thus bring kindness to the battle with another's belligerence. Yes, the tender-heartedness of the true Christian is most often born out of hurt. Out of his own sorrow, met and conquered by the kindness of God, he knows how to comfort another's sorrow. Out of his own disappointments and failures, by the grace of God, he learns how to help another rise out of his low spots to victorious living. Having felt the kindness of God, he is eager to share it with others.

The second characteristic of the kind Christian is his clemency in his judgments of others. Let us not confuse clemency with weak condoning of another's faults. The clement man learns his secret from God. He probably knows what sin is and the weight of its guilt, along with the supreme peace of forgiveness. In his dealings with the faults of his fellows, he seeks above all else to lead them to the forgiveness he has found. Even in the moral surgery which is occasionally necessary in dealing with sin, harshness can be avoided and hurts assuaged. The most complete frankness I have ever known, and the most helpful, is the frankness of the kind. How it disarms one's defenses and reduces one's tendency to resist help! If there is clemency in one's criticism of another, he can be even more frank, and hence more valuable, than can the harsh critic. Neither honesty nor moral forthrightness is Christian unless it comes from the clement heart. How clearly we see the difference between the Pharisees and our Lord in dealing with the woman taken in adultery. No less than they, he sees her sin and does not condone it, but it is his kindness and not their brutal righteousness which leads to her forgiveness and restoration.

A third thing about Christian kindness is its singular lack of concern for being paid back. Since kindness is love in action, the kind man is not concerned about himself, but about the object of his kindness. Unlike the do-gooder, he seeks no recognition, no praise. Indeed, he is usually surprised when someone notices his kindness. His good deeds are not for the gratification of his own ego, his own sense of power, or his own self-esteem, but solely for the person who needs what he has to offer. He is kind to the unkind if he is truly Christian, and he goes on being kind even when his kindness is met by cruelty or disdain. He is bound to be that sort of a man if the love of Christ possesses him. When filled with the love of Christ that is the inner spring from whence flows our imperfect kindness, the more we become possessed by him, the closer we can keep to him, the kinder we shall be. How kind he was, how kind he is to all the sinful men who nailed him to his cross. What sensitivity he has for your needs and mine. How kind are his judgments and how clement he is in his treatment of the sinner. How little he regards his own safety and his own self-importance. Yet, in that kindness, more than in anything else, he won men then and wins men now. No single virtue of the Christian has the power to draw others to the foot of his cross as does this one. Men are won to him by your kindness and mine more than by anything else, and kept away by our lack of it. "Be ye therefore merciful as your Father also is merciful" (Luke 6:36).

26

Is Morality Relative?

IN THAT often asked question, is revealed the moral confusion of our times. Time was, for the Christian at least, when an absolute moral code was taken for granted. He might not live up to it, but there was no doubt in his mind that the law was there, fixed and unchangeable, and that violation of it led to inevitable consequences. It is not necessary for me to tell you that the world in which we live does not subscribe to such an idea, and that because we live in such a moral climate, we find it increasingly difficult to maintain, both for ourselves and in our judgments of others, the traditional Christian pattern of fixed and absolute standards which are everywhere and always the same. This moral relativity of our times has not sprung up suddenly. It is rather the end of a process which has been going on for some time, accentuated by war and the prevailing materialism of our scientific age. We can't get at any real answer to this question until we determine what, as Christians, we mean by morality.

Is Morality Relative?

In the first place we mean something much broader and more inclusive than what has come to be understood by our common use of the term immorality. Just who is to blame for this dangerous narrowing of meaning, so that it applies only to one sin, I do not know. Certainly, man has one of his major battles with the primal urge of sex, and it is perfectly obvious that any moral standard worthy of the name must tackle that urge and bring it under control. But isn't it a bit curious, that even when one thinks of the question I began with, he is tempted to say, "Ah, the dean is going to talk about sex!" If I recall correctly, there are nine other things in the basic Judeo-Christian moral code of the Ten Commandments which are supposed to be equally important. Strangely enough, our Lord didn't spend too much time talking to people about sex. Maybe that was because his ministry was entirely to Jews for whom the sanctity of the family was second only to the sanctity of the temple. The one or two things he did say were blunt enough. In the Sermon on the Mount he told his listeners that anyone who looked upon a woman to lust after her had already committed adultery in his own heart. There can be no question that our Lord saw lust for what it is, a sin of both flesh and spirit. Foolish indeed would be the Christian who tried to say otherwise.

But it is interesting to note that morality, to our Lord, involved much more than it usually means to us. And it was man's failure in certain other respects which both incurred his strongest condemnation and finally nailed him to the cross. Here it might be well to be reminded of the six other deadly sins which the theologians have culled out of the teachings of the New Testament, and which Christians so easily forget. They are as follows: anger, gluttony, covetousness, envy, sloth, and pride. Just the listing of these sins ought to be enough to jar us out of our sense of moral relativity. For here, simply put, and on a par with the lust of the flesh, is enough to send every last one of us to our knees. Dorothy Sayers, the brilliant and gifted English churchwoman who, with C. S. Lewis, has done so much to restate Christian truth in terms our world can understand, calls the first three, lust, anger and gluttony, "warm-hearted and disreputable sins," and the last four, covetousness, envy, sloth, and pride, "cold-hearted and respectable sins," and states quite frankly that because the last four are so respectable, our Lord despised them most—not because they are more deadly than the first three, but because most of us fail to recognize them for what they are, or considering them relatively less important, are more apt to be guilty of them, to be harmed by them, and to do harm by them. It is right here that we begin to understand why this question arises in our mind. That you and I take much less seriously the sins of envy, covetousness, sloth, and pride than we do lust or violent anger, is an indication of our answer to the question. Yes, morality is a relative matter for us, if that is the way we feel about it.

A quick look at these other deadly sins will broaden our

moral thinking and make us less inclined to be guilty of placing such relative emphasis on some more than others. Uncontrolled anger masquerades as moral indignation which justifies every violent partisanship known to man and every war he has ever fought. Being a sin of the emotions, it inhibits clear thinking, causes us to do many things which corrupt our social existence, and feeds the fires of hatred and intolerance which ever and anon render society apart.

Gluttony, in its most vulgar form, is manifested in garbage pails piled high with wasted food and mountains of empty liquor bottles. We of North America are probably the most gluttonous people in history, save those of ancient Rome. Millions of our starving fellows at home and abroad could live on what we throw away. And our gluttony goes even further; we are caught in the fearful merry-go-round of our industrial civilization based upon our gluttonous consumption of the products of the machine. It is our sin of gluttony and its attendant greed that has delivered our world over into the power of the machine. The more the machine produces the more we have to consume, until we become overstuffed with things, and then find ourselves in a situation peculiar only to our age, that strange anomaly of want in the midst of plenty.

Covetousness, or avarice, is seldom recognized for what it is. It sometimes masquerades as honest thrift, enterprise, business efficiency, free competition, and enlightened self-interest. It is not incarnate in individuals, but in business corporations, which as someone has said, have neither bodies to be kicked, nor souls to be damned, nor hearts to be appealed to, either. It is the peculiar vice of individuals and groups who have much and want more. It is the mother of ruthless competition and of the gambling fever. Covetousness is one of the two deadly sins our Lord spoke most bitterly against, because in many respects, along with pride, it is the key sin of all. It is certainly the key sin of our generation.

Envy, the twin of covetousness, is the sin of those who have not, and resent those who do. It hates to see other people enjoying things. It, too, has its masks by which it passes as the virtues of right and justice. Its two great expressions are my rights and my wrongs. At its best, envy is a social climber and snob; at its worst, a destroyer, preferring to make everybody miserable rather than to have anyone happier than he. It is cruel, jealous, and possessive. It takes as dupes the generous-minded seekers after justice. Envy does not know how to admire or respect or be grateful.

The sixth deadly sin is sloth. It is defined by the dictionary as laziness or indolence, but is much more than that. It includes that indifference, which in the world masquerades as tolerance, but which in reality is nothing more than despair. To cite Dorothy Sayers again, it is the sin which believes in nothing, cares for nothing, seeks to know nothing, interferes with nothing, enjoys nothing, hates nothing, loves nothing, finds purpose in nothing, lives for nothing, and only remains alive because there is nothing it would die for. It uses all the other sins which preceed to cloak its emptiness. It covers up its mental indolence by spurious business. It is the peculiar vice of the disillusioned years which follow in the train of war.

Finally, and most important in the Lord's view, is the sin of pride. Volumes could be written about it, but the essence can be expressed in one simple statement. Pride is the sin of trying to be as God. It walks our world under the guise of two familiar doctrines, that of the perfectability of man, and that of inevitable progress. Pride turns man's virtues into deadly sins by causing each self-sufficient virtue to issue in its own opposite. It attacks us at our strong points, not at our weak. It is preeminently the sin of the noble mind, of the idealist, of the good, of the pious. As T. S. Eliot puts it in one of his plays, *Murder in the Cathedral,* "Sin grows with doing good. . . . Servant of God has chance of greater sin and sorrow, than the man who serves a king. For those who serve the greater cause may make the cause serve them, still doing right."

I think you can see now the answer to our question, is morality relative? It must be, for the real Christian at least, a reluctant no. I wish it might be less reluctant for all of us. But when we see morals for what they are, concerned with every single thing to which our bodies, minds, and spirits are prone, it becomes neither relatively simple nor relatively important as to which sin is worse; they are all deadly. They all get us off the track, and the end result is the same, no matter which sin or combination of sins besets us. Unrepented, often persisted in, they kill the soul. There are seven deadly sins: lust, anger, gluttony, covetousness, envy, sloth, and pride. They seldom attack singly. Like wolves, they run in packs. There is nothing relative about any of them and there can be nothing relative about our efforts, with God's grace, to conquer them.

27

Morality Begins in the Home

IF A belief in a good God who wants goodness in his children must lie at the heart of moral living; if, in other words, God comes first, then it is equally certain that the family comes second. Since morals have to do with the way in which we live together with others and the estimate we have of ourselves, the place where we first begin to learn and practice the good life is in the home.

The Jews through the centuries have understood this as no other race or people; it is no accident that one of their greatest glories is the quality of their family life. Nor is it an accident that immediately after the four commandments which do put God first, comes the positive commandment to "honor your father and your mother . . . that it may go well with you, in the land which the Lord your God gives you" (Deuteronomy 5:16).

For the Christian this ancient conviction of the importance of the home is equally basic. It is basic theologically as well as morally. It was in the family life of his race and out of his experience in the carpenter's home at Nazareth, that Jesus gained his great insights into the nature of God, God's relationship to mankind, and man's relationship with his fellows. The great concepts of the Fatherhood of God and the brotherhood of man are concepts drawn from Jewish family life. Intensely personal terms these are, which lie at the base of our faith as Jesus gives it to us. Therefore we can't even know what God is like or what constitutes our true relationships with others apart from the experience which a good home alone can give.

It is not surprising that the ebb and flow of real religion, the moral tone which it produces, is vitally and intimately connected with the quality of family life. So if there is a breakdown of morality in the vital religion essential to living the good life, then we must look for one of the basic causes of this unhappy fact in the breakdown of the home. However, rather than join the chorus of those who beleaguer the parents of our day, let me approach the problem positively as I try to indicate what a sound family life should be.

First, as the fifth commandment so clearly implies, the integrity of the home depends upon the relationship between the husband and wife. Before ever God gives them the privilege and responsibility of parenthood, there must exist the prior privilege and responsibility of the love shared by man and wife. In this divinely ordained relationship lie not only the seeds of the next generation, but the seeds of all the

Morality Begins in the Home

attitudes required if men are to dwell together in unity. Nowhere else in human experience is it given to man to come as near to experiencing the love of God, and nowhere does man come nearer to sharing in God's creative power.

That this relationship involves the expression of sexual desire, only fools deny. But suffice it to say in this connection, that while the relationship between man and wife certainly includes the physical, and is nourished by it, there is much more to a marriage than biology. As a younger priest influenced by the new emphasis upon the importance of sex which came after World War I, I used to say that I never knew a couple to break up if their sex relationship was right. I certainly cannot say that now after all these years of marriage counseling. The heart of marriage is not biological, the sharing of desire and the begetting of offspring. Desire becomes less demanding with the passing years. Children grow up and leave the nest, and biology becomes a pretty frail reed to lean upon as the years go by. There is nothing more pathetic than the middle-aged couple who go on living together, going through the motions of marriage, but as far apart as complete strangers. To be husband and wife requires infinitely more than pleasure in bed. Marriage requires the ability to communicate with each other, the joy of shared experiences of mind and spirit, the serious attempt to understand another human soul, the capacity to give and take, the resolution of differences without rancor or resentment, and the respect for another's personality which resists the temptation to make it over. Fundamentally, a truly satisfying marriage is nothing more than a firmly growing friendship, subject to all the requirements which enable people to live, work, play, and aspire together. And if this be not the only basis of moral living, then I know not the meaning of the term.

All of this gains added significance in the experience of parenthood. The fifth commandment is directed at children. They are to honor their parents. Honor is a mixture of respect and awe which issues not only in obedience and attendance, but with the passing years, in gratitude and filial love. But while this commandment seems to be directed at children, it certainly implies that the parents must be worthy of honor. And central to that worthiness is what the child sees in the relationship between his father and mother.

Often I've been called into a youth guidance center to confront some rebellious teenager. The case record almost invariably shows that the child feels he is not loved. Sometimes this is pathetically true; there are many instances of parental neglect in prosperous homes as well as poor ones. But often the evidence would seem to belie the child's feelings. He may have an exceedingly conscientious mother and an exemplary father. Why, then, does such a child feel unloved?

If one digs deeply he discovers a curious thing. The child feels unloved because he doesn't know what love is. He doesn't know because he has never seen it exemplified in his parents' attitudes toward each other. This is a devastating truth. Parents too often find a substitute for the love for each other in their love for their children. So wives become maternal slaves and husbands work themselves to death to provide advantages for their children. But the child instinctively sees through this, and failing to see the love relationship working between his father and mother, he becomes rebellious and a problem, playing the inner hostilities of parents one against the other, feeling unloved in his heart, because the primary relationship of the home, upon which all other relationships depend, has no love in it.

Frankly, I suspect that this weakness of the heart in modern family life is as responsible as anything for the modern cult of child-centeredness which, beginning in the home, has now pretty well taken over in education. As people fail in husbandhood and wifehood, they tend to become hyperconscientious in parenthood, with the result that the home tends to revolve around the child. So togetherness and palsmanship take over, and the child soon gets the impression that the family exists primarily for him. And the trouble is that even marriages which are soundly based to begin with can be harmed, sometimes irrevocably, when the child takes over. And even more important in the long run, the child misses the most important fundamental of moral living which is learning that in this world, his own ego and his own desires must be seen in reference to those of other people. Since his first contact with society is in the family circle, if he does not learn this there, how can we expect him to be a good citizen and a good Christian later on?

So amid all the emphasis upon the importance of a growing child, I would like to put in the plea for the importance of his parents. Parents have rights too. They are entitled to some privacy. They are entitled, by virtue of years and experience, to have opinions and set standards and expect the child to abide by them. Since disappointment and the inability to have one's own way are important factors in moral living, what is so wrong about a child's learning how to meet these things in the home? Since law is essential to our ordered society, where else can the child learn the importance of rules and the results of disobedience than in the home? Certainly, he will be a little monster at times, he will rebel and talk back, he will try his will against another. This is part of the growing-up process too, and must be recognized as such by wise parents. But self-discipline is an acquired art, born out of discipline imposed by some external authority. And when that authority is based upon parental love, it has a much better chance to result in self-discipline than the loveless disciplines society will impose later on.

It is perfectly obvious to you as well as to me, that one cannot exhaust this all important subject in one brief sermon. I have not had time to speak of the way in which prejudices, hopes, ideals, honesty, and kindness are learned in the home, not to mention attitudes toward religion.

What has concerned me primarily here is to get the whole

matter of the home and family in larger perspective. No generation of parents in history has been more self-conscious, more susceptible to expert opinion, more appalled by its responsibility. Why is it that in spite of this, so many of us fail to do as good a job as our grandparents who never had Dr. Spock or the child psychologists, or all the youth organizations, or the extracurricular activities we demand of our schools?

Maybe we are taking ourselves and our parental responsibilities too seriously and not taking our marriages seriously enough. Certainly, there are too few of us, even among Christians, who remember and practice our religion in our homes. For if the home is parent-centered or child-centered, and not God-centered, it cannot perform the divine function which the home of a simple carpenter in Nazareth performed long ago when Jesus was a boy. This is why God sets us in families: that in the tiny microcosm of the home, men may learn to live as morally responsible people in the great big world.

28

Making Marriage Work

THE final prayer of the marriage service is one of the most beautiful prayers in the prayer book. More than that, it sums up in a few brief words the goal of Christian marriage and what it takes to achieve it. In this brief prayer, we ask God to look in mercy upon the man and the woman who have made their vows that they may love, honor, and cherish each other and live together in faithfulness and patience, in wisdom and true Godliness. Why? In order that their home may be a haven of blessing and peace.

Every time I read that prayer it is with an earnest hope that something of its meaning gets through to those for whom it is offered, because I know, from my own experience, that it takes a lifetime to understand the meaning of that prayer. No young couple can be expected to do more than grasp some slight idea of its import. The excitement and nervousness which are almost always a part of a wedding are not conducive to deep thought and prayer at the altar. The main desire at that moment, I find, is to get it over with and get out. So the minister's words come through in a haze of emotion. With most couples, it is only when they attend the first wedding after their own that the impact of the service comes through.

Let's look first at the objective and purpose of a Christian marriage as stated in that prayer. That objective is one and one only—the creation of a certain kind of home. In other words marriage is something other than a legal contract which balances the rights and duties of both parties. It is something more than a socially acceptable means of permitting a man and woman to share the same bed. It is something more than a necessary adjunct to the procreation of our kind. And it is certainly more than a futile attempt to prove that two can live together as cheaply as one. All of these together cannot give marriage an adequate and enduring purpose. The true purpose of marriage is the creation of an environment which brings the blessing of peace not only to those who participate in creating it, but to anyone whose lives they touch. This is what a Christian home means, a haven in the turmoil and stress of life where refreshment can be found and strength given to go out again into the busy world better able to cope with its problems.

The achievement of this kind of peace doesn't just happen. Since it begins with two people, it first involves a mutual effort to create between themselves a relationship of peace. Every couple that has achieved it knows it is not easy. Like heaven, it is not reached in a single bound, but by a lifetime process in which the four qualities mentioned in the prayer are constantly operative.

The first quality is faithfulness, an old term which means altogether too little in this crazy age. What does it mean in a marriage? Obviously, it means the will and the desire to see it through, to keep one's vows, to be loyal to each other come what may. Faithfulness is, if you will, the glue that couples a man and woman in marriage. Without this complete commitment the marriage comes unstuck. Society no longer puts on the pressure to keep a man and a woman together. The pressure must come from within themselves if their marriage is to endure. Faithfulness then means an irrevocable decision to give oneself completely in love for the other, whether rich or poor, sick or well, in good luck or in bad. Ideally it is a mutual commitment, but in the last analysis it is an intentionally personal responsibility as I learned from observing one woman in my youth whose handsome husband fancied himself as God's gift to women. Affair after affair continued over many years, and, of course, it hurt her. But when my father, who was her pastor, suggested that she leave him, she said, "no, I married him for keeps. He's just as attractive to me as he ever was. I love him, and in his self-centered way, he loves me enough to come back each time he strays. I'm not responsible for the inadequacies of his love, but I am responsible for my love for him. Therefore, I'm sticking till death do us part." She did. In her long final illness, he never left her side and was devastated when she died. Was she a fool? Most modern women would say she was. But she knew what faithfulness meant, and in the end that faithfulness redeemed her man.

The second quality is patience. Ah, there's a tough one! At least for the likes of me. The need for patience begins as a couple leaves the altar and continues for the rest of their lives. Patience is first tested in all the adjustments newlyweds have to make as they learn how to live together. Little mannerisms, ways of doing things, from toilet etiquette to table manners, become trials of patience. Learning to love each other physically often requires as much patience as does anything else which is an art. Without patience there cannot be established that acceptance of each other as persons which is so essential. Without it little hurts become big ones, and minor matters blow up out of all proportion. Nothing requires more patience than the care and rearing of children. And lacking it, children become a curse instead of a blessing. In these days of two-career couples and single-parent families, there is an even greater need for patience with children. Both mothers and fathers run low on patience, and when they are exhausted at day's end they must be aware of the need to divide their emotional and physical energies between home and business. Patience is required every step of the way, throughout middle life when both men and women undergo emotional and physical changes, and into old age when absentmindedness and slowing down present new problems. Without patience no marriage can endure.

We come now to the last two qualities which make for a Christian home, the first of which is wisdom. Neither faithfulness nor patience is possible without putting one's mind to work in a marriage. Unfortunately, marriage is looked upon so much as a matter of subjective emotion that it never occurs to many couples that it requires intelligence too. It's a sad fact of my pastoral experience that men and women, with brains and a great deal of common sense which they apply to every other relationship, will use so little wisdom in their life together. People don't *think* about marriage. They emote and act like fools in the one place where wisdom is so needed. Wisdom means the ability to bring some objectivity into life together. It's sharing each other's thoughts, listening to each others' criticisms and suggestions without getting defensive, functioning as a team instead of working and living at cross-purposes.

Wisdom also means the capacity both for self-knowledge and knowledge of one's partner. In a right marriage the two go hand in hand. For example, I could never have made considerable progress in overcoming a tendency to self-pity and hypochondria if it were not for my wife's wisdom. Wisdom means knowing when to speak, and how and when to keep one's mouth shut; when to go for a walk at a tense moment, and when to put your arms around your beloved and laugh; when to put the children into their place and when to let them be the center of attention. It is knowing the art of

Making Marriage Work

give and take. It is, above all, the sharing of ideas, experiences, enthusiasm, and interests. The story of two women, both intelligent, both attractive, both religious, and both with difficult husbands is much to the point. One had a husband who was antisocial and liked nothing better than to work on a ship model or play a quiet game of cribbage. As the years went by, cribbage ceased, and while he was working on his ship model, she was upstairs playing bridge. Out of charity, she invited a divorcee friend to convalesce from an illness in their guest cottage. The guest began playing cribbage with her husband and tying knots in the rigging of his model ships. Of course, she walked off with the husband! The other wife was married to a rich playboy whose only real interests were photography and hunting. The wife came to me in desperation, and when I asked her whether she shared his hobbies, she said, "heavens no, I get claustrophobia in his darkroom and I am terrified when a gun goes off." I suggested to her in all seriousness that she had better grab hold of the only two handles she had and make herself like photography and shooting. She became a skilled assistant in the darkroom rather quickly. A year later, she asked him to take her to the fairgrounds, but wouldn't tell him why. Mystified, he did so, only to be thrilled to see his wife step up and win the women's pistol shoot of California. She not only kept her man, but he settled down to business and became a useful citizen.

Finally, marriage must be characterized by true Godliness. I like to stress that word, *true,* because there is a phony Godliness which has little meaning or value, the commonest example of which is finding no place for God in your life together except on Sunday at church. In my younger years, I used to say that there was no marriage insurance equal to kneeling at the same altar and going to church together. I still think it is important, but I've known too many couples who have done this whose marriages ended in divorce. True Godliness is something more than going to church together and then living the rest of the week as though there were no God at all. Sure, you teach your children to say their prayers and maybe grace before meals, but do you say your own prayers? Do you dare to try praying together when tension mounts and problems arise? I use the word, dare, because most of us are even more self-conscious about prayer than we are about sex. And it is sometimes more difficult to kneel down together beside a bed than it is to get into it. Speaking of sex and prayer in the same breath may seem shocking, but it shouldn't be. Nowhere do we need more to put God into the marriage relationship than in the physical side of it. Leave him out of that and intercourse never becomes what God meant it to be, a sacramental act, the outward and visible sign of the inward and spiritual desire to be one with one's beloved. Without true Godliness, neither faithfulness, nor patience, nor wisdom is possible, and marriage itself fails to bring the blessings of peace in a truly Christian home.

29

Love, the Basis for Moral Living

OUR purpose in this sermon is to try to find a basis for moral living which is both realistic and Christian. Realism and the gospel of Jesus are not contradictory. No one has ever been more realistic about man and the human scene than was Jesus. Actually, he was too realistic, too clear, and his conclusions were too simple for his contemporaries to grasp. They still are, for man has a way of complicating the truth and beclouding the issues, all in the interests of that pseudo-profundity which is associated with religious belief and practice.

The only purpose of Jesus is to show his fellow men what manhood is and what God is like and what he wants us to be. He calls us to grow up, become mature beings, free from slavery either to one's own passions or to a supposedly jealous God. But some of us don't want to grow up. If we still believe in God, we continue to think of him as a hard taskmaster or an eye in the sky whose critical gaze watches our every move like big brother in George Orwell's *1984,* or as a celestial bookkeeper, keeping our accounts, or a stern judge meting out justice to a perpetual delinquent. There is much fear and no joy in such a faith, as I know well from my own youth. Such faith produces a most unneighborly attitude that is spiritually and morally adolescent, and ignorant of the maturity and freedom that is in Christ.

The strong moral freedom I have spent a lifetime trying to find, roots in one basic attitude toward oneself, one's neighbor, and one's God. It is all summed up in the great commandment of Jesus, that I love God with all my heart and soul and mind and love my neighbor as myself. Love is the key word in that commandment, but love is the most inadequate important word in the English language. We give it many different meanings; we confuse it constantly with that other word, like, when we describe our pleasure in a beefsteak, in a game of golf, in a symphony, or in a work of art.

Love in its truest sense always involves personal relationships. Yet even here the word is inadequate. The Greeks were much wiser. They had three words where we have one. Eros was the natural carnal drive of the sexes for each other. Philos described the relationship between friends or within one's own family. Agape was considered to be the highest form of love, and described the relationship between man and God, and eventually between brothers in the family of God which is the Church. Erotic love in its natural form is

Love, the Basis for Moral Living

self-controlled. In man it is not. Of all loves it binds itself most easily to desire to possess for one's own gratification. Being fundamentally self-centered and possessive, it is the cause of jealousy which is one of the most insidious poisons of the human spirit. Rooted in the body and driven by instinct, it can possess the mind and the soul as well. Natural and God-given it certainly is, but if erotic love be not caught up in the higher loves Christ is talking about, man becomes much worse than the animals. The higher expressions of love, philos and agape, have one thing in common which erotic love does not have. Whether used to describe the love of God or of man, they both imply an earnest and anxious desire for the well-being of the one who is loved, and the willingness to make that well-being come true. Unlike erotic love which seeks to possess the object of its affection, these higher loves seek to give of oneself to the object for the sake of the one loved.

Let us see how this works out in the three areas included in Christ's one and only commandment. That commandment is directed to each of us personally. You are to love God, your neighbor, and yourself. We tend to overlook the place of the self in all of this. To imply that there is such a thing as a proper and necessary self-love, seems on first thought to be completely contrary to the selflessness which we always associate with Christ. But, is it so contradictory? I think not. The self is the whole being of an individual—body, mind, and spirit. And it is with this whole self that Christ asks me to love God and my neighbor. If any part of me is held back, my ability to love is reduced by that much. If my mind gives intellectual assent to truth which my spirit does not feel and my body does not act upon, that truth means nothing. If my spirit is captured by a great and strong emotion, untouched by thought, I am bound to say and do many strange and harmful things. If my body's natural appetites get out of hand, uncontrolled by mind or spirit, I debase myself to something lower than an animal.

The achievement of selfhood is, after all, the main purpose of existence. Who am I? Why am I here? How can the conflicting parts of me be organized into a unified whole? The quest for identity is what modern psychiatry calls this, but whatever it's called, it lies behind the rebellion and experimentation of youth and the frustrations and failures of age. Each of us wants to be free to be himself, but the question is which self?

It is right here that the first and great commandment comes into play. I cannot decide which self I want to be until I give the disorganized, warring incompetent me to God in whatever act of love I am capable of giving. As a youth I was afraid to do that because I was afraid of the God whose commandments I had broken and whose will I had thwarted. When finally, in my senior year in college, I decided to gamble on God's love, I'm afraid it was penny ante with a ten-cent limit. But that small venture paid off, and as the years have increased, so have the stakes. Perhaps some day before

Love, the Basis for Moral Living

it's all over, I shall have the sense to go for broke as Christ asks me to do. But in this long process, I have learned some very important things about myself.

I know that I cannot give anything worthwhile to others which I do not myself possess. I know that I cannot act responsibly toward others unless I act responsibly toward myself. I must be friends with myself if I am to be another's friend. I must grow in my love for God if I am to help others know and love him. I cannot help to clean up a dirty world or bring a sense of forgiveness to a mixed-up soul with dirt in my own mind and unrepented wrong on my own conscience. I have learned that my own morals, or lack of them, begin inside of me, as Jesus said they did. I no longer blame my failures on others; they are my failures and mine alone. I may not have been responsible for the warping of myself as a child, and knowing how I was warped and why, certainly helps. But I can no longer afford the cheap luxury of using these alibis. For at the heart of every failure is a failure in my love of God and in my understanding of the dimensions of his love worked out in the business of living.

So far I have been very personal, but what applies to me applies to every one of you. The well-being of your own self is terribly important in the whole field of morality. Therefore, to the young I would say, your self-centeredness, your rebellion, your doubts and questionings, and your desire to experiment is part of the process of growing up as a person. It is not an easy process either for you or for those responsible for you. But it is the only way in which you can begin the struggle for maturity. It is well to remember that physical maturity comes much earlier than mental, moral, and spiritual maturity. Be not deceived into the assumption that because your bodies are ripe, this makes you a whole and complete person, ready to live with a responsible freedom. You need not believe this just because I say so. You can find out the hard way if you want to, but there is, alas, plenty of evidence around you in the pathetic mixed-up older people you will meet, whose bodies are mature and minds are well trained, but who simply have not grown up spiritually. Not having learned to love, they drive love away. Not knowing God, they know neither themselves nor their neighbor. Is this the kind of person you want to be a few years hence? Do you want to carry around in an adult body an adolescent soul confused, unstable, inadequate to meet life's situations, unable to make moral judgments which are sound and right? Of course you don't, nor need you. But for the moment it is well that you observe the ground rules to which experience over the centuries has given some validity. They may change a bit here and there, they may seem silly or unnecessary at times, but if ever you are to learn the moral self-discipline of free and mature persons, it must begin that way.

And to those of you who are older, I would suggest that morality, like anything else, is something which is best passed on by example rather than by precept. I remember the father who was terribly upset because his teenage son was in juvenile court for stealing. But that same father, one day at the church door with his son standing beside him, boasted of the slick trade he had finessed on a new Cadillac after turning back the mileage on his old car. If a mother's object is to dress to look sexy, how can she expect her daughter not to do the same? A father's roving eye is perfectly obvious to his growing son, and his dirty stories are sometimes the only impression he ever gives his boy about sex.

But more important is the quality of love our children see in their homes. It is no accident that the children of broken marriages are more apt to fail in their own. If they never see the love whose primary purpose is giving for the sake of the beloved, if husband and wife are not good friends but enemies, how can they be expected to see in this greatest of all human relationships, something of precious and enviable value?

I must close even though my task is far from done and, I am afraid, quite inadequate. It was fool-hardy to assume that it could be otherwise in so short a time. Yet, if I have accomplished nothing more than to disturb some, and to help others to do some hard straight thinking about morality, rather than drift with every wind that blows, then by God's grace some little thing may have been accomplished. As I grow older I cannot forget the rules pounded into me in my childhood and youth. I am grateful now that there were some rules then, as there too often are not now. But they are now my rules, not Moses' rules nor my father's nor those of the

Church. Some of them I have long since abandoned because they were not moral precepts, but mores of the society in which I grew up. I can dance, or play cards, or go to the theatre without thinking it a sin. Free from tension and grimness, free to go on experimenting with the wonder of God's love for the likes of me, free also to see my actions and my relationships with others not as compulsions of duty, but of love, there is joy to be found in trying to live the good life. It can never be a perfect life, and the need for repentance and forgiveness grows as the awareness of love's meaning grows.

So I close with the words of Paul. "Rejoice in the Lord always, again I will say, Rejoice. Let all men know your forbearance. The Lord is at hand. Have no anxiety about anything, but in everything by prayer and supplication with thanksgiving let your request be made known to God. And the peace of God, which passes all understanding, will keep your hearts and your minds in Christ Jesus. Finally, brethren, whatever is true, whatever is honorable, whatever is just, whatever is pure, whatever is lovely, whatever is gracious, if there is anything worthy of praise, think about these things" (Philippians 4:4).

30

The Pursuit of Happiness—The Promise of Joy

Happiness is a universal desire of humankind. In the Declaration of Independence, Jefferson classed the pursuit of happiness along with life and liberty as one of the goals of human effort. He was announcing no new discovery.

There is only one disagreeable thing about happiness and that is, the harder we look for it, the less chance we have of finding it. As a result, the pursuit of happiness makes more unhappy people than almost anything else in this world. Like any other valuable thing in life, happiness is a byproduct. It is not something about which we may say, "now I am going to find happiness." Rather, it is something which results through forgetting the pursuit of it; something which is added to man's experience only if he seeks the highest and best life of which he is capable. That is the real wisdom of why happiness never comes to those who make it their main goal of life.

Pleasure is another thing we want. It is natural for all

living things, from the single-celled amoeba to man, to avoid pain and to seek pleasant feelings and experiences. But the trouble with man's hunt for pleasure is its unnaturalness and artificiality. Not satisfied with simple earthy things, we resort to all sorts of stimulants in the quest of a good time. We flog our jaded bodies and lazy minds with artificial arousements, with the result that the very pleasures we seek and pay millions for become empty ones. Strangely enough, happiness and pleasure are for many the chief aims of religion. You will find that to be true of the numerous success cults which have flourished in recent years which guarantee peace and prosperity, sweetness and light as the result of their faith. You'll even find it in the churches where the test of spiritual vitality is too often put upon the ability of a preacher to titillate the ear of the sermon-taster, of the choir to give good entertainment. We need to be suspicious of any religion which holds out happiness as the chief bait. We need to be suspicious of our own religious quest if happiness is the chief thing sought. Jesus never said we'd be happy if we followed him. Rather, he offered us a cross to carry, a burden to bear, and a load to lift. He could not have said anything else, for the pursuit of happiness, in religion as in life, is selfish through and through.

There is, however, a quality in vital Christianity which the non-Christian mistakes too easily for happiness. That quality is what the New Testament calls joy. It is so important an element, that on the basis of the New Testament, the gloomy

The Pursuit of Happiness—The Promise of Joy

Christian is a contradiction in terms. Our Lord himself, in spite of the obvious defeat which awaited him, met life gladly. That was one of the things which bothered the long-faced Pharisee most. That a man could be religious and still be the life of the party, that he could be dignified and play with children as a little child, that he could preach and live a difficult, cross-laden life with a smile, was a new experience for those men for whom anything that was fun was wrong. Religion for the Pharisee was deadly serious. It never allowed a man to unbend to enjoy hardy laughter or the sparkle of ready wit.

How then was Jesus' daring promise of joy fulfilled? You will find the story in the closing chapters of the four gospels. It began with a faint glimmer of light in the darkened souls of his friends on Easter day. With each new evidence of his risen presence, the light grew until it burst into full radiance on Pentecost. And all through the book of Acts of the Apostles, that radiance of joy persists. It enables Paul and Silas to sing hymns at the top of their lungs while bound in chains in prison. It enables St. Paul, the converted Pharisee, to rejoice in his afflictions. The word, joy, is repeated again and again in his letters. The joy of the Lord was a real thing in those days.

It was this radiance that captured the ancient world. The Roman Empire was beset by a nameless growing fear which produced at its best the grim humor of the stoic with his "grin and bear it" philosophy, and at its worst, the synthetic artificiality of the epicurian, "eat, drink and be merry for tomorrow we die." But in early Christianity, stoic courage and epicurian gaiety were combined in a new way. Only the Christian could face the worst a chaotic and cruel world could do with that reckless selfless courage which had in it a place for a smile and a song. The Romans had seen lots of brave people die. They had never seen them die singing hymns of praise to almighty God.

If we examine the joy of the Christian, whether then or now, we shall discover at least two things about it. In the first place, Christian joy is rooted in unselfishness, unlike the pursuit of happiness. The gladness which possessed the disciples after the resurrection was a gladness about Jesus, not about themselves. Sure they were glad that he could still be with them as their risen Lord, but they did not attain the fullest joy until they stopped reveling in his presence after his ascension. Then it was that they were happier still for his sake. His seeming defeat had ended in victory; his untimely end had proved to be the beginning of a far greater story, the last chapter of which has not yet been written.

The thing which happened gradually in those forty days after Easter was that these men stopped thinking about themselves. They began to think and to care only about Christ. He became the only one that mattered. I wonder if that is not the reason we know so little about what happened to the twelve with the exception of Peter, James, and John. The others drop out of the New Testament picture completely. Might not the reason be that Jesus and his gospel became so important to them that their selfish pursuit of lasting fame receded into the background as they tried to make Jesus king in the hearts of men?

Yet here we are, so many of us casting envious eyes about us; coveting power, position, wealth; trying in various futile ways to find happiness. What fools we are, when for almost twenty centuries we have had available to us the one true formula of joy. The thing that matters is not what life can give us, but what we can bring to it. It matters not if our little lives are unsung and soon forgotten so long as through us Jesus may continue to live in men's hearts.

The other thing we can say about Christian joy is that its background is the cross. Put it any way you like, explain it any way you will, it is impossible to know what joy is unless you know what pain is. In one of the most vivid passages of the gospel we are told that Jesus, after the resurrection, showed the disciples his hands and his side, and the writer makes what seems to be an astounding statement—that the disciples were "glad" when they saw the Lord. How in the world could the sight of those fresh scars, so reminiscent of their own cowardice, make these men glad? I think I know why. Those wounds were the sign of their Lord's triumph over that very cowardice. And over the other sins that caused the wounds. A risen Christ without those scars would not have been their Christ. It was the agony of the cross that made the resurrection such an intensely joyful experience.

Don't we find that out in so many of life's hardest experiences? Ask a mother if any time of her life was as surcharged with joy as when she looked into the face of her first-born. In that selfless moment she forgets the pain for the joy in her child. Through sickness, through failure, through defeat, there comes to us so often the joy that seeks us through pain as it seeks us no other way.

Why then is the Christian glad? To begin with, he knows how real sin is. How it leaves its horrid mark upon both body and soul and leaves him with an overwhelming sense of futility and doom. Then, someone with nail prints in his hands comes into his life and replaces the reality of sin with the deeper reality of righteousness. Someone who heals the wounds Calvary has made and transforms futility into hope and gives life new meaning and value. Is it any wonder such a one is glad?

Here is another who has walked the stony road of doubt and fear and questioning, always seeking and never finding, until at last cold cynicism has laid its hand upon him and driven him to bitterness and despair, and someone comes into his life just as he did to Thomas long years ago and says, "Put your finger here, and see my hands: . . . do not be faithless, but believing" (John 20:27). And in the revelation of the simple fact of the eternal truth that is the Christ, his doubt melts away and he cries out, "My Lord and my God" (John 20:28). Is it any wonder why such a one is glad?

Here is yet another who stands beside the lifeless body of

a loved one seeking helplessly to do what little can be done for all that is left to honor. Then that someone walks in the dark garden of sorrow and speaks a word of comfort as he did to Mary long ago. The grave becomes a sign of hope, and life is lord of death. Tears of mourning turn to tears of joy because he lives; we too shall live. Is it any wonder why such a one is glad?

Wonder no more. Seek no longer for the passing elusive shadow you call happiness. Give your life with all its ambitions, sins, doubts, and fears to him. Lose your life in his life. Forget yourself. Remember only him and your needy brothers and sisters and then you will know the peace of God that passes all understanding; joy that no man can take away from you.

FOUR

And it is my prayer that your love may abound more and more, with knowledge and all discernment.
Philippians 1:9

31

God in the Garden

Lord of all power and might, . . . Graft in our hearts the love of your Name; . . . nourish us with all goodness; and bring forth in us the fruit of good works" (Collect, Proper 17, *The Book of Common Prayer*, 1977).

One of the things I miss most in apartment-house living since my retirement is the joy of working with growing things in the garden. I didn't always like gardening; it was my wife, Faith, who taught me to love it, and in our years at the deanery, it became for me the activity which fed my soul. Of course I wouldn't be much of a gardener now. If I got down onto my knees to weed and plant and grub in the good earth, someone would have to help me to my feet. About all I could do is prune, but I still miss it.

There was one rose in the deanery garden which was exceptionally beautiful. Not being an expert in rose culture, I used to wonder why every now and then a stem would spring out of a root which produced very ordinary flowers, quite different from those I particularly admired. Then a rose fancier gave me the answer. The flower I had admired had been grafted on the sturdy root stock of an ordinary rose, and every now and then the strength in the root would spring up and fulfill its natural destiny. The man who wrote the collect quoted above must have been a gardener; he likens the Christian life to a grafted plant in which the sturdy stock of our humanity, joined with the beauty of God's grace, produces a finer product than our own humanity can achieve. This analogy, like many others we use to describe the fusion of human and divine, contains a truth of great importance.

In the first place, it indicates God's reliance on the stuff of our humanity as the root and base of Christ-like living. We do not often think of it that way. We conceive of our human nature as somehow quite different from God's. It is not. We possess his capacities in a rudimentary form. We intend, we will, we think, we love, even as God does, and we also share in his creative power. The Bible makes this quite clear, and nowhere more so than in the life of Jesus our Lord.

When God sought to enter the life of man be began with man himself. He did not begin all over again. He used the sturdy stock of our humanity as the base for a new creation. Quite logically he chose the stock of the one race which had a genius for religion—the ancient Hebrews. More than any other people they had reached toward him, and in reaching had achieved a moral and a spiritual stature none other had. And even more important, the Jews possessed a spiritual hardiness which had survived every hostile environment one could imagine. It was a tough stock indeed.

So, to a Jewish peasant woman was born a child; that child trained as a carpenter, became the one we know as Jesus. Flesh of our flesh, bone of our bone, the roots of his indomitable character ran deep into the life of man on this earth. Tempted as we are, subject to our limitations, being born, living and dying as we do, this is the often forgotten earthy fact upon which our religion is built. This is the root stock of humanity from which the flower of the gospel draws its nourishment. Jesus is our Savior because he is the Son of Man.

You and I ought to remember this when tempted to despise our humanness. God needs the earthy stuff of our mortal natures to produce the flower of the gospel, and no small part of the glory of Christ's likeness is its dependence upon man's own nature to achieve it. So upon this stock rooted deep in the good earth, capable of producing flowers similar to God's, is grafted the divine stock. Grafting involves skilled surgery, the cutting and splicing of the new to the old, and the patient care of the surgeon until the graft takes. Always there is the danger of rejection of the new body as in the transplanting of human organs. If the graft doesn't take, then the potential beauty of God withers and dies on the human root, which survives and continues to produce inferior flowers.

The analogy is quite clear. The process of conversion,

whether it be sudden or slow, involves surgery even as grafting does. One does not become a producing Christian without some pain. Take love for example. Our collect prays that love for God may be grafted into our hearts. Each of us possesses the capacity for love, even if only to love ourselves, but human love is partial and limited at best. The other side of love's coin is often prejudice and hatred as it rejects the unlovable, the different, and the unfamiliar.

When the love of God impinges upon such human love, it demands hard things of a man. It does things to his egotistic impulses; it forces his capacity to love into new and strange channels, it broadens his perspective, for in showing God's love, he is required to do what God does, love the unlovable, the different, and the unfamiliar. This is the true religion the collect sees as the result of a successful graft of God's love upon our human love. True religion is more than creed or ritual or church. It is far broader and far harder than that. These very things which we so easily mistake for true religion are very much like the band placed around the graft which, when fixed too tight, chokes the merging of the human and divine so that the graft doesn't take. Likewise, many a conversion process is aborted when one mistakes these things for the end result. Love does not flow within us when the grafted stock withers and dies. But, as the collect clearly states, after the grafting takes, the divine human plant must be nourished. It must be watered and fertilized and cared for all the more because it is a fusion of two similar yet different

God in the Garden

kinds of life, each dependent upon the other, yet both together producing the desired result.

We often assume that once the conversion process is completed there is nothing more to do. Alas, that is not true as I know too well in my own experience. The conversion process is never completed; it goes on and on and on throughout one's life-span obeying the laws of growth. Occasionally the hardy old human stock of the root bypasses the graft and sends up a rank but flourishing shoot which behaves for all the world exactly as one behaves without God's love. It is then that we need the divine gardener to take his snippers and cut it off where it joins the root so that the life-giving sap may flow where God means it to flow. Surgery never ceases in this business. Pruning must be done. Dead stalks which have served their purpose must be removed if new flowering is to take place. The plant must be shaped so that light and air can join with water and food to produce the flower.

Far more than the culture of the rose, the culture of the life of God in the body of man requires unending attention all our life through. This is what my garden taught me and this is what this collect means. Weeding is a part of that culture, pruning is essential. Pests must be eradicated; all those little irritating things which stunt and mar the life of God seeking to express itself in you and me. When the winter of doubt, disappointment, and sorrow holds us in its cold embrace we need the protecting comfort of the mulch of God to keep our roots from freezing. This is where the practicality of prayer, purposeful meditation, and self-criticism come in. This is why we worship. It is all necessary to keep the life of God flowing within us.

32

Life's Ups and Downs

THE man who first called the Sunday after Easter, low Sunday, must have had a sardonic sense of humor. I suspect he may have been a parish priest, or perhaps a cathedral dean, who could not help noticing the contrast between what goes on that morning and that of the previous Sunday. Perhaps this use of the word, low, was a reflection of his own mood, his own letdown after the excitement and intense concentration of Holy Week and Easter. But whatever the initial reason, calling it low Sunday does indicate a very intelligent insight into the inevitable ups and downs of life. Things never stay the same for long. The sun rises and sets, the moon waxes and wanes, the tide ebbs and flows, season follows season in unending procession.

It would be surprising indeed if man, the child of nature and the child of the God who made nature, should be exempt from the invariable law. Nor is it alone in the physical aspects of man's life that we see this law at work. It is just as applicable to the intellectual, moral, and spiritual side of our being. There is, for example, a constantly recurring cycle in the mental development of the child. At times the acquisition of new knowledge and the avidity with which he goes after it is so intense and so rapid that we are amazed at his progress. Then, there follows a period of seeming stagnation, of downness and indifference to knowledge, of disinclination to study. How troubled parents are when they discover that the intellectual brilliance of yesterday has become the dullness of today.

The same is true in a child's moral development. There are times when the moral issues of childhood can be met and conquered easily. When telling the truth and being kind, cooperative, and thoughtful seem to be the natural expression of a child's whole personality. Then everything seems to slip backward. There is a constant battle between the moral ideas of the parent and the perfectly devilish little barbarian who cannot seem to get them at all.

Precisely this same process goes on in a man's spiritual life. At certain high and holy moments, God seems so near that we could reach out and touch him. Our whole being is suffused with a new strength, and our senses are attuned to new insights into the nature of God and our relationship to him. In such moments it seems as though we could never wander very far from his presence again, or never drop back to the self-centered, materialistic level of lesser days. Then that great moment passes. The vision departs, the presence

Life's Ups and Downs

fades, the thrill is gone, and the hard realities of life beat in upon us persistently and disturbingly. In vain we try to recover something of that which we felt in the great moment.

How clearly all this is brought out in those vivid pictures of what happened to the disciples following the resurrection. If one were not so familiar with such an experience it would be difficult to understand why it took so long to convince those men and women that Jesus was risen from the dead. During the forty days following the resurrection, their faith went up and down. When he was with them they believed and were sure. When he left them they began to doubt. Even St. Peter, who had seen Christ with the others on the day of his resurrection, became so discouraged that he gathered the ex-fishermen together and went back to the old task on Galilee. In short, the apostles themselves had the same sort of cycles in their faith and religious experience that all men must have.

This common experience of human variability has troubled religious people more than anything else. If you will read the lives or personal journals of the great saints, you will discover that the rise and fall of their religious feelings and insights concern them much of the time. One of them called it dryness of the soul, the stopping up of the wellspring of religious devotion, the parching of spirit under the arid winds of doubt and discouragement. Perhaps it will come as a shock to some of us to find that the finest Christians in all ages had their low moments, and that most of them lived for weeks, months, and sometimes years without being able to recover the thrill of the great moment of illumination which had started them on the road to sainthood.

The first thing we should recognize about these troublesome reactions which are apt to follow some high moment in our religious experience, is their naturalness and universality. Such recession of spirit is as natural as our changing moods or physical letdowns. And because it is natural, it also serves a beneficial purpose which we would do well to recognize. For one thing, our nervous and emotional natures can no more stand prolonged spiritual excitement than they can stand any other kind of too-long sustained excitement. It is just as possible to be exhausted from a great joy as from a profound sorrow. When a man worships God with his whole being, as we are apt to do on high and holy days, his nervous system is, as it were, stretched taut, and relaxation afterwards is vitally essential, and being vitally essential, it is in the law of our nature inevitable.

Furthermore, this reaction following exaltation has a distinctly religious value. Our re-enjoyment of the great moments and high days is dependent upon the little moments and lesser days for that contrast which gives the former their value. If all our days were equally thrilling how monotonous religious experience would be. That is why I firmly believe that the people who value Christmas or Easter most are not those who come to church solely on those sacred days.

To worship in the church only at the great festivals is to

get a false perspective on this whole matter of the Christian life. It is also to miss the ebb and flow of the Christian seasons with their periods of preparation and anticipation. One does not catch the total spirit of the family at a big formal party. One learns the meaning of family life only by being a member of it, by sharing its downs as well as its ups, its discouragements as well as its hopes, its sorrows as well as its joys. And the same is true of God's household, the Church. It's true of this whole business of trying to follow Jesus Christ.

But the danger for each of us lies not only in the temptation to discouragement, but in the tendency to accept our letdowns as the norm of Christian living. Each of us, while enjoying the excitement and exaltation of a great day, is by nature a spiritually lazy mortal. And each of us is always looking for a good excuse to relax our efforts as much as possible. Therein lies the great difference between the great Christians we have called the saints, and most of the rest of us. There sainthood is demonstrated, not because of some great vision seldom vouchsafed to lesser men, but because they had the courage and faith to walk in the light of that vision when, like lesser men, they were tempted to give in to reaction. Take St. Peter, for example. He messed things up pretty badly when, after the last supper, he denied the Lord. But he refused to take his denial of Jesus as the norm he wished to follow. He went and wept bitterly, but he was also at the tomb early on Easter morning.

So it was with Francis, and Catherine of Sienna, and Augustine, and Wesley. So it has been with others. They refused to accept their lowest ebb as the measure of their capacity. They kept right on praying when God seemed far away. They kept right on believing when hopes were blasted. They kept right on with their religious exercises whether they felt like it or not. The trouble with most of us is that we do not do this. We give in to our religious moods, because the heavens do not always open and God does not seem so near. We rest back in supine contentment with mediocre piety and easy living, and then we wonder why the great vision doesn't come. It can come only when we walk by the light we already have. It can come only when day in and day out, in depression and in exaltation, in defeat and in victory, we keep true to the insights we already possess.

33

The Forgiveness of Sins

IT IS no accident that the only teaching of Jesus that is written into the Church's creed is the teaching of the forgiveness of sins. It is not an accident, because more than anything else that he ever taught, forgiveness answers man's deepest need. The wages of sin weighed heavily upon the ancient world. For the Jews, the God whom they worshipped was an exacting God, hedging life round with the infinite details of the law so that one was in perpetual danger of transgression. Among the rest of the people of the Greco-Roman world, there was a great weariness which demonstrated itself not only in fatalism, but in a pervading desire to seek release in artificial pleasures and debaucheries. It was from these states of mind that the religion of Jesus Christ redeemed men, and continues to redeem men, if they give it a chance.

Before we can talk about forgiveness, we must see more clearly what it is for which we are to be forgiven. The first question therefore that we must consider is the all-important one—what is sin?

We find many definitions of sin in the Old and New Testaments. To the orthodox Jews, sin was breaking the law, that infinitely detailed body of restrictions which only the Pharisee could hope to keep. The ordinary Jew in Jesus' time had developed a hopeless attitude and despaired of his capacity to keep the law. Another meaning of sin is missing the mark. Of all the definitions of sin, this would seem to be nearest to the experience of most of us. We see what it is we want to accomplish, we think we have the means, yet our using of those means is so imperfect that we come wide of what we intended to do.

Sin is also losing the way. Perhaps the clearest example of what we mean by this is to be found in the parable of the lost sheep. In losing our way, we are not only the victims of our own moral inadequacy, but we are also victims of our own lack of knowledge. People lose their way, usually when they do not know any better, even as the sheep wandered away from the flock. There is also, particularly in the New Testament, a concept of sin as living at less than our highest level. There isn't one of us who is not a sinner by this definition. Sometimes we are surprised at our capacities for moral courage and moral achievement in moments of crisis, only to find that afterward we seem to fall back to a level of living which does not put too much strain upon us. This tendency is so universal that the unused portion of man's moral nature is

The Forgiveness of Sins

one of the most colossal bits of waste in the universe.

In all of these definitions of sin, there is one thing which runs like a shoddy thread through the whole fabric of man's sense of inadequacy and that is the feeling of bondage. Again and again, St. Paul and other writers of the New Testament spoke of the enslavement of man to sin. Nothing could be nearer the truth in our experience. We want to do better, we want to rise to great heights of moral achievement, we want to lead the good life, yet when we start out to live it, we feel bound and gagged by something within us which prevents us from reaching our goal. I think you can see, therefore, that sin is something much more universal than the sins we ordinarily catalog such as adultery, murder, stealing, and lying. These things do not have the universal meaning for respectable people which accounts for the feeling of sin which most of us have at certain moments.

We need now to examine whence our sense of sin arises. In the first place, it arises from the imperfection of man's nature. One of the penalties we pay for the gifts of conscious personality is the awesome sense of contrast between the goal toward which we strive and the distance we come from achieving it. This is one of the weaknesses of our nature which we do not like to admit, particularly in the realm of man's social achievement. While we are terribly conscious of our own personal limitations, we like to feel that the things we do en masse are not subject to the limitations of persons. Therefore, we feel that the nation to which we belong is immortal. We feel that the institutions into which we pour our effort will somehow survive for eternity. That is, we like to feel this way, but when some crisis comes along and our institutions begin to totter, and our nation becomes afflicted with the concentrated sins of individuals, we are terribly disillusioned with the transitory nature of everything man does. There is, in other words, a partialness about all of our efforts. Just when we think we have achieved perfection, something happens to cast us downward again. We lived through that years ago when, following World War I, the greatest prosperity known up to that time crumbled, almost overnight, into the greatest depression in history. Then all the inadequacies in the structure we had built were revealed in sharp and disturbing outlines. The achievements we had attained became, in many instances, definite handicaps in the new situation of crisis. Even the wonders of modern science, which had contributed so greatly to our sense of material well-being, showed themselves capable of perversion by evil men. All of this is disturbing, but according to the insights of Christian faith, the imperfection and inadequacy of man's achievement are the best things that God in his wisdom has planned for us. Otherwise we should become so content with the things of this world that we would forget our eternal inheritance.

The second thing out of which our sense of sin arises is the conflict within us between that which is of the earth and that which is of heaven. You and I are citizens of two worlds, part of us is wedded to earth, subject to the limitations of the flesh and the appetites of the body. But there is also within us something which is not wedded to mere existence on the earthly level. The dreams, the hopes, and the spiritual ambitions of men have somehow been evolved out of the things of this earth, and the things of this earth cannot satisfy this other side of our nature. The sense of sin is the price we pay for being something more than an animal. We are not content to spawn and get our food and find our shelter and clothe our bodies and call it quits at that.

Another corollary of this is that the possibility of our sinning is the price we pay for the freedom of choice which God has seen fit to give us. In that naive story of the Garden of Eden and the first temptation, there is a tremendous truth—that the moment primitive man began to sense the difference between right and wrong, he began to be a possible sinner. Here again there are some things glorious in the divine plan. Take away the possibility of sinning, and the tremendous achievements of human virtue lose all their significance. Take away the possibility of sinning, and all of man's struggle toward the diviner things of life loses its values and appeal.

We turn now to an examination of the process of forgiveness. The Christian belief in forgiveness is founded not upon a need, nor upon logic, but upon experience. The Christian believes in the forgiveness of sins for one reason, and one only, and that is because through Christ, he has been forgiven. For almost twenty centuries that experience of forgiveness has been associated most intimately with Jesus upon the cross. Beneath all the theological arguments about the meaning of Christ's death, lies one true insight as to the sublime significance of that tragic event. The ordinary man is not saved by reasonable argument nor by noble philosophy. Only an intensely dramatic representation of truth will move him. The cross is just that. The acting out on the stage of history of the meaning of God's forgiving love.

The death of Jesus upon the cross is an eternal reminder of what man's sin does to both a good man and to God. As we think of the things which put Jesus there, we see ourselves in true perspective as participants in the age-old attempt to kill that which is good. We also discover that sin itself is a spiritual thing. St. Paul kept talking about the powers of darkness in heavenly places (Ephesians 6:12). And by that he simply meant that the only things which Christ reveals afresh are not just the sins of the flesh, but the sins of the spirit—the stubbornness which characterizes so much of our thinking, with its refusal to see new facts and face new truths; the prejudices which so completely dominate our lives that we are quite powerless to see the good in that which, for selfish reasons, we prefer to hate; the blindness which so often characterizes the attitude of otherwise good people, which keeps them from seeing the great signposts on God's highway as they go their willful ways to destruction; the indifference which cannot be bothered by appeals to lofty motives

The Forgiveness of Sins

and high ambitions which disturb the comfortable repose of comfortable people. These are the things which sent Jesus to the cross. These are the things which send Jesus to the cross again and again in human history. And until we can see exactly what our participation in this eternal tragedy may be, and ourselves for what we are in the light of what the cross reveals of human sin, we cannot take the first step on the road to forgiveness. Forgiveness involves a true perspective on ourselves before we can take the initial step of repentance.

And what is repentance? Repentance begins in the consciousness of our individual share in the contemporary tragedy which leads to genuine sorrow for our part in it. It is not enough to blame it on the other fellow, it is not enough to lay the responsibility for the sins of the world upon those whose ideas and methods we do not like. Repentance is a very individual thing, but it has social consequences, and there is no possible way by which the modern world can work out of the disorder which engulfs it until we, and all people everywhere, are willing to see ourselves as sharing in the world's sin and are ready to get down on our knees in confessing it.

The cross is a constant reminder, not only of what sinning man does to God, but of what God does for sinners. One of the most significant testimonies to the meaning of the cross in all the vivid gospel record, is the testimony of the Roman centurion. He was no pious fanatic, nor one given to great spiritual aspirations. He was a soldier, a rough and ready man, who had doubtless seen service on the farflung battlelines of the empire. He had seen men die so often that his heart must have been inured to death, yet this death was different. There was something in it which compelled his attention. There was something in it which transcended the very agony of death itself. The centurion had doubtless taken up this nasty job with a sneer upon his lips as he thought of the claims of Jesus reported to him by his fellow officers. But in the death of the man upon the cross, he realized that those claims were true and finally was forced to say, "Truly this was the Son of God" (Matthew 27:54).

On the cross we find no God of hate, no far-off deity of vengeance, no hard and exacting judge, but one in the person of that man, come down into a world of sin and tragedy, who turned defeat into victory and ignominy into triumph. That is the God that we see upon the cross. It is a God who suffers for and with his children, who can take of the very tragedy of sin and make of it the sublime truth of a new righteousness. As we look at that kind of God there is something within us which moves us irresistibly in his direction. He is the kind of God that we need, the one for whom we instinctively long. In the death on Calvary we find, more supremely than anywhere, that God truly was in Christ reconciling the world unto himself. This is the Godward sign of forgiveness. It is rigorous. It does not minimize the inevitable consequences of sin. There is nothing weak or sentimental about the story of the cross. It is rugged and instinctively demands the highest

The Forgiveness of Sins

type of effort and character on the part of those who are moved by it. It is the strong love of God that moves out over the waste of human sin and draws all men unto himself. *All* men, irrespective of race, class, or social position. *All* men, because all are the sinners for whom Christ died.

Finally, in the death of Jesus, we find the eternal reminder of what the forgiven sinner must do for other sinners. In the Lord's prayer forgiveness is conditioned upon our willingness to forgive. Jesus, of course, was not a sinner as you and I, but one of the most significant things he did in the last hours of his life was to demonstrate a willingness to forgive those who had done him injury. The thief beside him, the hateful priests, the jeering mob, the cowardly disciples—all of them were swept in by the breadth of his love when he said, "Father, forgive them for they know not what they do" (Luke 23:34).

I submit to you that if Jesus, the sinless, could find it in his heart to forgive those who had wronged him, how much more should you and I feel bound to forgive? Of course, we forget we are sinners when other men sin against us. We place them in a different category. We refuse to see similarities between their weaknesses and our own. But in so doing, we are aggregating to ourselves that which even Jesus did not dream of doing. He took unto himself all of the blindness, indifference, stubbornness, and prejudices of those sinful men and committed them and their sins to the Father's forgiving love. When we talk about the forgiveness of sins and claim it as our inalienable right at the hands of God, let us not think of it too lightly as something which God will automatically do for us. It is a promise with a condition, one of the hardest conditions man ever has to fulfill. But, if God himself can find it in his heart of love to save us from the bondage of sin, how much more should we pray to be able to forgive others their transgressions.

34

The Sin of Inferiority

Any normal person feels inadequate to life at certain times. If that were not so, we should be as God. It is when this normal feeling of inadequacy becomes an obsession, damning ourselves and our relations with others, that it becomes the sin of inferiority.

There is nothing wrong in and of itself in recognizing one's limitations. That is a mark of a mature person. Part of the process of growing up is the recognition that we are mortals, that there are some things we cannot be and do, and that God himself doesn't demand any more of us than our capacities can stand. But that is not what I am thinking of now.

The trouble with most of us does not lie in our failure to recognize the upward limits of our capacity. It lies rather in our tendency to live at the lower limits of our capacity. Few, if any of us, are living up to the best that is within us, either physically, mentally, or spiritually. At best, we shall be inadequate enough, but most of us are more inadequate than we need to be. The reasons for this are many. The laziness and inertia of mortal beings is partly responsible. There is something within most of us which is satisfied with getting by. Like the average student, we are content with passing grades, and are not interested in straight As.

But there is another and more subtle reason, and that is the tendency to judge ourselves and our varied abilities at the level of our greatest weakness. For example, the physical inadequacies most of us face in one way or another assume a continuing importance in our self-estimation. One of the greatest discoveries of the modern study of psychology is that the most frequent cause of an obsession of inferiority lies in a physical handicap, real or imagined. These bodies of ours are wonderful organisms, but they are not perfect. They are subject to accidents and disease, and they wear out through use. Superficially, also, they are not universally attractive. The Apollo Belvedere and the Venus de Milo are significant, not only because they are great art, but because they represent a standard of physical perfection few of us can attain. We can smile at these things, but the fact is that they are responsible for a lot more of our feelings of inferiority than we realize. The moment a growing personality becomes self-conscious, he begins to compare himself with others around him, and the first thing he is aware of is physical differences. It's tragic when a homely girl first discovers her friend is beautiful. There is no inward pain equal to that of a

The Sin of Inferiority

cripple when he watches the robust energy of other boys on a playing field. Whatever it is that we are conscious of as physical limitation becomes the standard of our comparison with others. And in that comparison we come off a very uncomfortable second best.

The same process takes place in other phases of our life. From the day a little child enters school, he is faced with the possibility of finding himself mentally unequal to his fellows. To be sure, that possibility, realized or unrealized, tends to require a healthy effort to keep up his grades, but the moment he gets the idea that he cannot keep up, at that moment, the healthy spur of a possible inadequacy becomes the disease of inferiority. In other words, feelings of inferiority arise out of other inequalities of life. A man out of work or harnessed to an uncongenial task, a childless woman, a brilliant mother tied so completely to the arduous chore of raising a family that she has no time to use her mental gifts, all these are easily overwhelmed by feelings of inadequacy.

But whatever the cause, the effects follow certain definite patterns. With some, there is a shyness, a shrinking from contact with others for fear of being hurt. With others, there is an agressive chip-on-the-shoulder approach to life, striking before another strikes, and facing life in a mood of belligerence. Both of these reactions produce unhappy and lonely people who make difficult friends and disagreeable companions. If sin is that which destroys our happiness and effectiveness and blights our relationships with others, then surely such attitudes toward life are sinful.

There would be no point in our discussion if we had to leave it right here. But we don't have to leave it right here. There is that in the Christian approach to life which can and does drive out of men this persistent and destructive evil of inferiority.

In the first place, the religion of Jesus with its emphasis upon a God-centered life rather than a self-centered life can lead us to the first step in eradicating this devil. That first step is knowledge of its nature and real cause. All these so-called causes of inferiority are not the real causes at all. The chief thing that ails most of us is an exaggerated sense of power or importance. The supreme egotist is not, as we might suppose, that rare person who feels superior, but that common person about whom we are talking. He is an egotist because most of his time is spent in thinking about himself. It makes no difference how low the estimate of himself may be, that has nothing to do with egotism—the point is that he is thinking about himself. Also, he is an egotist because he thinks everybody else is thinking about him. Put him in a room with other people and he imagines that every eye is looking for the flaw in his makeup, that every ear is attuned to his blundering speech. The truth is that none of us gets the attention he thinks he is getting. We aren't quite that important after all, and it is a healthy beginning to our conquest of inferiority to realize that. It may cause a painful deflation of our ego, but it is a healthy pain.

The Sin of Inferiority

The second step in this conquest is to recognize that a limitation in one direction is not a limitation in every direction. Most of us make that sort of discovery quite naturally; some find it more difficult. The psychologists call it compensation, and history is full of those who have more than made up for their limitations by excelling in other directions. Napoleon is a classic example of a little man who made up for his physical deficiency in military genius and power to command. Hitler is a modern example of the same thing. But in the case of these two and in other more common instances, I think we can agree that compensation is not enough. The trouble is that mere compensation does not destroy the conceit which is the product of a feeling of inferiority. On the contrary, it heightens it, and makes for that sort of strutting cleverness which men respect, and sometimes fear, but do not love. The world admires the man who wins out in spite of handicaps, it bows in homage before the self-made man, but in the long course of history, it has suffered more at his hands than at any others because such an egotist cares not one rap for anyone except himself and his own glory.

There is another kind of compensation, however. Long before there were any clever psychologists to coin the words which we use as though they represent some new insight never seen before, men had learned the secret of triumph over their infirmities. They found that secret in every religious faith, but supremely in the faith we know as Christian. Where Buddha found it in the denial of man's inadequacies,

Jesus found it in the acceptance of those inadequacies. He began by accepting his own: his lowly birth, his humble home, his meager education, and his cruel death. Every handicap known to man was part of his experience. That we have to make an effort to recollect Jesus' inadequacies is a measure of his triumph over them. How strong he seems, how impervious to the hurtful things of life. Not even the ultimate debasement of the cross could dull the radiance of his victory.

The secret of his triumph lay in his trust in God. He accepted from God's hands, as from a loving father, the glorious privilege of life. He saw the limitations of his manhood as the opportunity for victorious living. With no limitations to conquer there could not be for him, any more than for us, the thrill of victory. Further he sought from the inside that which faith alone can give, the right attitude toward himself. You remember that he asked the disciples who men thought he was. When they replied, Elijah or one of the prophets, he was not satisfied. He did not want to be an imitation of anyone else, a copy, no matter how grand, of another personality. He wanted to be himself in his own right, so he asked the disciples "who do you say that I am?" To which Peter replied, "You are the Christ, the Son of the living God" (Matthew 16:15). Christ accepted that description because he believed it was true; he did not falsify that answer the way many a swaggering egotist with an inferiority complex has done. He accepted it, lived up to it, and left it to

The Sin of Inferiority

the God-given insight of his followers to the end of time to discover that estimate to be true.

Praise be to God. He has passed on to his followers that heritage of victory. Beginning with Peter, the ignorant fisherman, and Paul, the bigoted Pharisee, men who have looked up to Jesus have lived way beyond their limitations. History is so full of examples that it is useless to cite them. From the humble women of the New Testament to Helen Keller, from those peasant disciples to Phillips Brooks, countless persons have, through faith in him, conquered their inadequacies, risen above their failures, and triumphed over sensitiveness without losing their humility and without conceit.

God wants us to be ourselves at our highest and best. He judges us not by comparison with others, but by comparison with what we might be if we would. He would not have us think less of ourselves than we ought to think. And we need, above all else, to remember that God looks not upon the outward man, but upon the heart. Not upon beauty of body, but upon radiance of life. Our fellow men do too, more often than we suppose. Both God and man ask only this of us, that we live up to our best. *Our* best, mind you, not *their* best. And if we do that, forgetting self and losing our lives in the living of them, we shall conquer our inadequacies and like St. Paul, be able to cry, "on my own behalf I will not boast, except of my own weaknesses" (2 Corinthians 12:5). Thanks be to God who gives us the victory through our Lord, Jesus Christ.

35

Three In One—One In Three

THE feast of the Holy Trinity is unique to the Anglican communion. Originating in Spain in the early Middle Ages, spreading through the Gallican church in France, it survived only in England. This festival of the triune God is dedicated not to the commemoration of an event such as Christmas and Easter, nor to a person such as a saint, but to a theological doctrine. Following the festival of the Holy Spirit, Trinity Sunday is logically dedicated to the task of pulling together the total experience of the Christian with the God whom he worships and adores.

There are many difficulties involved in the traditional doctrine of the Trinity. The arguments of the Church fathers of Nicea as to how one almighty God could be divided into three separate and distinct persons and yet retain his oneness, seems sadly irrelevant to the unphilosophical mind. It is inconceivable to us that fellow Christians could have fought so bitterly over the precise meanings of the word, and

Three In One—One In Three

then come up with the seeming contradictions of three in one and one in three. "What theological gobbledygook," we are apt to say and dismiss it from our minds. Most of us are neither philosophers nor theologians, but we are used to testing the truth of things through experiment and experience. This is what is known as the empirical method of arriving at truth, a method very much in harmony with the rational, skeptical, and scientific temper of our time. It is, if you will, the practical approach, and it is just as valid in understanding the nature of God as the nature of the atom. Let's apply it to the doctrine of the Trinity.

Let me offer two simple analogies. The sun which rises each morning and sets each evening affects our lives in various ways. It gives us light, heat, and equally important, invisible rays. A blind man would know the sun's heat, but not its light. A person with a rare malady which gives him no sensitivity to heat or cold would know the sun as light. Prescientific generations were totally ignorant of the invisible rays, while we take them for granted. But the important thing about this is that we are not dealing with three suns, but one, which we experience in various ways, whose diversity arises out of our experience, which is determined by our capacity to experience one, or two, or all three aspects of the sun's nature as it affects life on this planet.

Consider now a more personal analogy. As dean of a cathedral, you experience me as priest of the altar, as preacher in the pulpit, as pastor in the sickroom or study.

Each of these aspects of my ministry has a unique quality, and so does your response to it. But I'm also a husband and father, known to my wife and children in a way no one else can ever know. In addition, through the years I have been privileged to have a few close friends who know me in still another way. Allowing for a normal amount of schizophrenic complexity in my personality, the many-sidedness of a human being, it is really the same man making his impact in all these relationships, although experiencing each in different ways.

Like all anologies, these are not completely adequate, but they do give us a clue to the empirical meaning of the ancient doctrine of the Trinity. When I watch the sun set over the mountains or turn my eyes skyward to the stars; when I see the storm clouds flying on the wings of the wind, or marvel at the beauty of a rose; when the earth trembles in a convulsion deep within the seemingly solid rock, or the robin wakens me at dawn on a spring morning; it is God the Father, creator of heaven and earth who gets through to me in all his power and glory.

Then, when I pick up my New Testament and read again the story of a man by the name of Jesus, meditate upon his words, am stabbed awake by some new insight in his parables, am moved by the awful majesty of his death and the power of his resurrection, and he stands forth from the printed pages, real, as though I were there, again it is God who gets through to my mind and heart. Different, yes, in many ways to what I feel in creation, and yet the same power moving me to adore and wonder at the love of God. What is it that makes this possible? What moves me to respond to the mystery in nature and in Christ? What makes me, in spite of myself, or in spite of all my unanswered questions, be a religious being, a believer, a man of faith? What makes you the same?

It is out of such questioning that believing man has come to know God as the Holy Spirit, the God within his own soul, the God who is closer than breathing, nearer than hands or feet. The creed defines him as the Lord and giver of life and this is exactly what we know him to be. It is he who moves man to rise above his natural inadequacies to a stature unobtainable apart from God. It is he who vitalizes all our faculties, giving us power to be and do that which we could not be and do unaided by his presence.

This God within your soul and mine reveals himself in many ways. He is the God of the conscience, that mysterious monitor each of us possesses which enables us to make value judgments of right and wrong. Without him the conscience is an untrustworthy instrument, similar to a compass whose magnetic field has been disturbed. He is like the North Star, ever constant, ever true, ever giving the right course to our lives. He is the enlightener of the mind who, using the mysterious electrical impulses of our brains, enables us to think purposefully toward the right goal. He is the giver of insights beyond the normal results of rational thought, the source of the scientist's discovery, the saint's revelation, and the common man's capacity for recognizing something he has never seen before that enables him to say this is right, this is true, and to feel a heightened sense of something beyond his own power which drives him to his knees.

This God within works through our will, giving us the capacity to tackle impossible tasks, to make improbable dreams come true, to urge us on to goals from which no difficulty, no discouragement nor defeat can deflect us. Worlds removed from the natural stubbornness some men possess, this God-given ability to see things through can make the timid brave, the weak strong, the defeated victorious, and the dead alive. This leads to the holy daring of the prophets who, in Israel's dark years, alone, misunderstood, and often killed, spoke the truth as God gave them to see it. This God transformed those inadequate disciples of our Lord into the intrepid band who started his Church toward its long task of bringing the gospel into a lost world. And again and again in other dark years, he has raised up brave men and women who, despising the darkness and dangers of their times, have kept the light burning. And what the Holy Spirit has done, he still does today.

While the spirit of God dwells within and operates through individuals, the most amazing thing is that the evidences of his presence are usually revealed most clearly in a group of individuals. The contagion of God's spirit is phenomenal, eclipsing any other known to man. This holy virulence, this heavenly plague, possessing the personality of

Three In One—One In Three

a man, never remains in him alone. It spreads. It is communicated to others. It leaps from soul to soul, irresistibly and inevitably. This is why the experience of the Holy Spirit becomes most obvious when Christian people come together with one accord in one place. It is God's will that no man hug to himself alone the things God gives him to know and experience. It is by sharing this Holy Spirit with others that the gift grows. It is the value in communicating, one with another, by song and prayer and sermon which justifies getting out of bed of a morning to come to this church.

To be sure, the vitality and significance of what happens when Christians come together depends upon the vitality which you and I bring to our common worship. Not always does the fire strike and the light shine and the spirit move us with equal force. Just as not always is my soul or yours fully attuned to the promptings of God, just as the disciples, after their Lord appeared to them for the last time, met every day for nine days before the mighty power of Pentecost swept over them, so we must often wait for the spirit's power to move in and through us. God the Holy Spirit is unpredictable. "The wind blows where it wills, . . . but you do not know whence it comes or whither it goes; so it is with every one who is born of the Spirit," says Jesus (John 3:8). Perhaps it is not God, but *we* who are unpredictable. I do not know, nor does it matter too much if in constancy, expectation, and patience we wait for him in faith.

Whether this Holy Spirit, this God within, proceeds from

the Father or the Son is relatively unimportant. For me this God who, at times, moves me to deep awe and wonder at the power and beauty of creation, speaks to my human need through Jesus Christ, or brings me suddenly to life, seemingly from within my own mind and soul or in a worshiping group of which I am a part, is one God, known in various ways, experienced in differing situations. For purposes of clarification of my thinking or description of my experience, it is useful to call him Father, Son, and Holy Ghost. But he is the same no matter how I try to describe him. He is a great God—too great for any human mind to explain or classify completely. But he is not too great to worship and adore as Lord and giver of life. This is the heart of Christian faith, the cause of our devotion, and the goal of all our striving.

36

Religion's Part in War and Peace

RELIGION has always been an exceedingly useful instrument of warfare. That is true of all religions—Islam, Confucianism, Shintoism, Hinduism, Judaism, and Christianity, both Catholic and Protestant. It is particularly true of religion in its organized and institutional form. Church and synagogue, mosque and temple have resounded through the centuries to the sounds of marching feet.

It has been the custom in recent years to criticize the institutions of religion for their part in war. More than one veteran has told me that he believed the declining power of organized religion is the inevitable result of the betrayal of the world at the hands of holy men who should have known better. Unfortunately, there is a lot of truth in such a criticism. All one needs to do is to read the war-time sermons of ministers, priests, and rabbis in every country involved on both sides of a great struggle to discover that organized religion has done a pretty thorough job on behalf of Mars.

Pulpits become recruiting stands, altars become places where priests call for blood, even as they did in ancient times, and congregations implore the deity for victory over the enemy.

Yet, such criticism is bootless if it fails to take into account certain things, inherent both in the nature of organized religion and in the society of which it is a part, which tend to make such a betrayal possible. First, a religious institution is an integral part of human society. It is not isolated, cut off from the tempers of mind and emotion which move through the rest of society. The men and women who belong to it are not church members only. They are also businessmen and professional men, republicans and democrats, parents and teachers, employers and employees; they are influenced by the same propaganda by which the non-member is influenced, and are moved by the many and diverse claims of conflicting loyalties which characterize our complex social order.

Furthermore, because the Church is one of several basic institutions of society, its welfare is closely bound up with that of other basic institutions such as the home and the state. If one of these is threatened, it is quite natural for man to assume the others are equally in danger. Man seldom fights solely to preserve his country. He fights to save his home, and if his church means anything to him, he fights to preserve that as well. Sometimes he fights to preserve organized religion even when he gives no other evidence of being seriously concerned about its welfare.

Religion's Part in War and Peace

If all this affects the attitudes of people inside the Church, it also affects the attitudes of society toward the Church. The state expects certain things of organized religion, even in a country like ours, where Church and state are supposed to be separate. In times of peace it expects the Church to urge people to be good citizens. In times of internal emergency, it expects the Church to support its policy and program. But in times of war, the state not only expects, but demands the support of the Church. The men who run the state have learned through the centuries that to have organized religion on their side is a tremendous asset. If you can cloak the brutalities of warfare in the mantle of religion and identify God's cause with the cause of the state, half the battle has been won. A sort of innate idealism within the human breast inhibits one's fighting instinct unless one can be convinced that he is fighting a holy war.

And strangely enough, it is right at the point of this innate realism that organized religion and deeply religious men become drawn into a betrayal of their divine trust. For religion sharpens the moral sense of man just enough to make him keenly aware of that which threatens the moral basis of society. His very idealism makes the religious man peculiarly prone to a deep concern for the establishment of those ideals. He is moved to what he likes to call "righteous indignation" at injustice, inhumanity, and brutality on the part of individual, group, or nation. Convince the religious idealist that he is fighting to free the slaves, or to make the world safe for democracy and he will become the most ardent champion of the use of armed force. Convince him that the aims of warfare are good and that they represent the will of God, and if attained, will bring in God's Kingdom upon this earth, and he will be the most intense and dynamic protagonist. Popes and monks leading the armored knights into the crusades against the infidel, Martin Luther supporting the German nobility against the rebellious peasants, Cromwell splitting the heads of English royalists in order to bring in the divine commonwealth—all these were idealists, convinced that God's will could be attained by force.

In other words, war has been and still is considered by many believers in religion to be an effective instrument of religious policy. Frankly I'm not half so concerned over what the military may do to lead us into war as I am in what I and my fellow religionists may do. The men who have fought have no illusions in the matter. They know that in the muddy hell of the trenches, the lofty ideals preached from pulpits seem quite irrelevant and remote, and the men who are charged with the preparation of our armed forces have no illusions either. They see war in terms of such realities as nuclear missiles, biological warfare, bombing planes, and mechanical equipment whose sole purpose is efficient death. Because of the danger of war as an outgrowth of the very idealism and moral sense which religion engenders, I want now to consider religion's place in the pursuit of peace.

That involves certain things which organized religion

must get clearly in mind and keep there constantly. In the first place, religion must remember that good ends are never attained by bad means. Jesus once said you can't gather grapes from thorns nor figs from thistles (Matthew 7:16). To illustrate, let me ask two rhetorical questions. Was the world made safe for democracy back in 1918 or in 1945? No, of course. Again, did the last war prove to be the end of all war? Listen to the guns in Lebanon and Cambodia and count the billions now being poured into armaments, and what must our answer be? No, of course. I cannot be cynical over the maimed bodies lying in the streets of Beirut; these are awful realities which wring the heart of any normal human being. Nor can I be cynical as to the need for a recovery of international honor and integrity. But I am convinced that maiming and killing men, women, and children in the crowded streets of Beirut are not going to make such murders impossible in the future nor restore order to an anarchic world.

If we must have wars let's see them for what they are. Men and nations fight for one of two reasons—to protect what they've got, or to get what they need. And both of these reasons are fundamentally selfish. Jesus may have been wrong when he said, "Whoever would save his life will lose it" (Mark 8:35). He may have been indulging in a bit of whimsy when he said, "Blessed are the meek, for they shall inherit the earth" (Matthew 5:5). Nevertheless, he did say these things, and it would seem to be incumbent upon those who profess to follow him to seek with all their might to prove him right.

In the second place, organized religion needs to be vigilant on all occasions for those positive contributions it can make toward the attainment of peace. It is not enough to do what I have already suggested, unless to that realistic approach toward war can be added an equally realistic approach toward peace. The collapse of idealism during recent years has clearly demonstrated that the passing of resolutions and the signing of treaties cannot guarantee peace. Resolutions and treaties have value only when they are backed by the will to peace and by the moral integrity of governments and people. In one sense there is no such thing as the moral integrity of a nation. For a social group, even if it be as large as a nation, is but the projection on a wider scale of the moral integrity of its individual citizens. If enough individuals in that state are selfish, the state will be selfish. If enough of them believe that the end justifies the means, so will the state. If enough of them hate, suspect, and fear their fellows, the nation will do likewise.

It is precisely at the point of the individual's attitude that religion has its major opportunity and its greatest challenge. It is almost trite to say that our modern world is suffering from a breakdown of moral strength and spiritual insight. Men and nations need to recover the lost values that once were considered plain ordinary morality, but are now considered amusing relics. We need a rebirth of plain honesty.

We need a new sense of charity and unselfishness. We need a focus upon God to save us from seeing this earth as a charnel house of self-destruction.

Because these things are the things we need so badly, I must go on believing that the hope of the world lies in the very things in which every high religion believes in its best moments. I believe it is the duty of the Church of Jesus Christ to hold aloft, as never before, those things which her master sealed with his own life's blood on a Roman cross. I believe it is religion's duty to elevate, and not prostitute to base uses the latest idealism of ordinary men who, in their better moments, catch a glimpse of the high road to God's Kingdom. I believe that the Church owes a terrible debt to those she has sent out to fight and to die, and that she cannot discharge that debt unless she does her best to maintain, in the midst of a mad world, at whatever cost to herself and to her leaders, the ancient verities of justice softened by mercy, responsibility touched by unselfishness, and moral vigor tempered with love. Of those of you who are outside the Church, I beg that you always be aware of her responsibility and grant her the freedom to discharge it. Of those of you who are inside the Church, I beg that you may not forget the tragic lessons of the past and may hold steadfast in these trying times. Steadfast in the faith that God still rules, that the nations of this earth are in his hands, and that ultimately, with man's help, "his Kingdom may come, his will be done, on earth as it is in heaven" (Matthew 6:10).

37

The Gift of the Spirit

WITHOUT the gift of the Holy Spirit, no one of us can live an effectual Christian life. That is a blunt statement, but Christian experience proves it to be true. The scriptures call the Holy Spirit a gift because that is exactly what it is. Even though manifested most clearly and definitely within our life and character, there is always something about the Holy Spirit which seems to come from without. Often unsolicited or unexpected, never wholly earned or deserved, yet there it is: a gift, which our instincts tell us, comes from a vital source outside ourselves. There is no way of predicting how or when this gift shall be given. Even the disciples, waiting in the upper room twenty centuries ago, did not agree as to just how they knew the gift had been given. To some it seemed like a sudden warmth and brightness, as of tongues of fire dancing in the room. To others it sounded like the rush of a mighty wind filling all the house. That first gift of the spirit came to some men and women meeting together in a group. They were meeting in a familiar place, probably that same upper room where the Lord had shared his last meal with his disciples, and to which he had returned after his resurrection, to convince them he was alive. That upper room was to them a holy place, full of precious memories and deep associations. It would be easy to explain what happened on the basis of group psychology were it not for the fact that others, in other times, have received this gift alone in unfamiliar surroundings, at most unexpected moments, with none of the encouragement of a group. Some have received the gift in the midst of sin, despondency, or bitter rebellion and have become great saints like Paul and Augustine. Others, like Brother Lawrence, have felt the spirit rush in at the sight of a barren tree in winter, or amidst the ordinary routine of housework or business. Still others have received it while glimpsing the sunset or a mountain, or listening to the steady roar of the sea. Even the cry of a baby or the laughter of a child are avenues whereby the spirit enters our souls. The point is, the gift of the spirit is from God, and since his wisdom and power are infinite, the "how" of his gift is infinite too.

Yet whether one receives the gift of the Holy Spirit as a member of a group or in some moment of extreme solitude, there is one thing which is common to all who receive it, and that is a definite sensation of something beyond oneself moving in upon one with a power. Be it only one brief moment, or a longer period of time when the spirit comes, he lets us know of his coming through the very sensory means by which other experiences impress themselves upon our consciousness. Then it is one sees the light that never was on sea or land, or hears a sound more beautiful than the ear has ever heard, or feels in tingling nerves the very touch of something more real than any earthly object.

Suddenly, in the midst of our occupations, whether at work or play, the beyond breaks through into the here. We feel a catch in our throats, or our bodies are subfused with a new warmth, or our eyes suddenly fill with tears as we become aware, in that moment, of something we have never known before. A new vision assails us. We see ourselves and others in a new light. And possessed of new insight and new power, old habits, old doubts, and old fears fall away and we feel clean and released and ready for some higher adventure.

I doubt if there is anyone who has not had some such experience at least once in his life. But perhaps some of you have had the experience and didn't recognize it for what it was. It is important that you recognize it for what it is and not dismiss it as some momentary self-induced hallucination or vagueness of the mind. It is the almighty God, in whom we live and move and have our being, who is trying thus to reach us through the avenues of our senses and the illumination of our minds, and foolish are we, indeed, to fail in our awareness. That gift, misunderstood or refused, may not be offered again. The heightening of spirit passes, the vision fades, the insight becomes blurred and indefinite unless we do something with it to justify the giver in giving.

This is what our Lord meant when he called the sin against the Holy Spirit the one unforgivable sin. To be given insight and turn back to blindness, to be shown the way and turn aside into some easier bypath, to be granted new energy and then dissipate it in doing something less than the will of God, that is the supreme tragedy of the human soul. For the gift of God's spirit carries with it an awesome responsibility which to neglect eternally means to fail eternally. That is the unforgivable sin.

But when one receives the gift and acts upon it, there are certain unmistakable and universal signs which can be observed, not only by those who know what to look for, but also by those who know not. The first indication of the appropriation of the gift of the spirit is a changed life. You can call it by the old term, conversion, or by any term you want. But when God's spirit moves into a human personality, everyone knows something has happened. They may not know *what* has happened, but they certainly know something has. We see that so clearly in the record of Pentecost. The small group of ignorant and humble men and women, nobodies in the Jerusalem of almost two thousand years ago, whose only claim to distinction was a questionable and foolish loyalty to a young rabbi who was crucified by the Romans a few weeks earlier, became on this day, the talk of the town before sundown. Gone were their self-pity, their fears, their doubts, and their feelings of inferiority. Ignorance had become the highest knowledge, doubt the deepest certainty, and their fear the most amazing boldness. They were changed, converted, made new by the gift of God's spirit. A new life shone in their faces, a new confidence rang in what they had to say, a new humility replaced the craven manner of the nobody.

That sort of thing has gone on happening to people ever since. It happens now; it can happen to you. Let no one tell me there is anything nebulous about the Holy Spirit. I have seen him shining in the very face which was once hard or dissipated, discouraged or bitter. I have watched him transform the defeated life into the victorious, the selfish into the selfless, the hate-filled into the love-possessed. I have known him to heal broken relationships and to assuage sorrow's tears. These are facts, my people. Facts as glorious and convincing as anything that happened to the disciples or the fanatical Saul of Tarsus. Men and women can still be changed, thank God. Here and now. Today.

There are yet two characteristics of the spirit-filled life which I want briefly to consider. The first is that the gift of the spirit, if it is real and acted upon, provides a guiding light which makes change permanent, leading the converted soul upward and onward to new heights of character. The guidance of the spirit works within the normal processes of our nature. It stimulates the mind so that the very thinking process itself becomes subfused with divine insight and character. We see this at work in the record of the New Testament, where not only Paul the scholar, but Peter the fisherman, think with the mind of God and choose the will of

God. Again, the spirit stimulates the conscience, that otherwise interest-worthy monitor, which sits at the gate of will. Without the guidance of the spirit how easy it is for conscience to betray us with its rationalizations and stupid blind spots. But when the spirit possesses us, the conscience is stirred to new keenness and perception, and instead of being in the main a negative monitor saying *stop*, it becomes a positive force saying, this is the way, *go*.

Finally, the spirit-filled life is an enthusiastic one. That enthusiasm need not be noisy or overdone, rather it is more often quiet, deep, and restrained. But I have never known anyone to be conscious of the gift of the spirit without being so everlastingly bubbling over with gratitude that he is bound to share it with others. It was the contagious enthusiasm of that small group in the upper room that swept like wildfire through the ancient world. And it is still the same. For today the good news of Jesus is spread by contagious enthusiasm and by no other way. But it is an enthusiasm born of the spirit and of nothing else. I covet this gift of the spirit for myself more than anything else. If in our worship and our fellowship, we wait and pray expectantly, may God give us a larger measure of his spirit, and the grace to use what is given to his honor and glory.

38

The Meaning of Sainthood

EACH of us is concerned about death. Whether we admit it, deny it, or postpone thinking about it, ultimately we are forced to consider it. The fact of death is here, waiting to be reckoned with, soon or late. In this respect the sophisticated modern, comfortable in his home, is no different from his pagan ancestor, digging in for the winter in the forests of northern Europe. It is simply easier for us to postpone the reckoning. Death is a mystery, even as life is a mystery. Every religion known to man has to reckon with death, and with life, in order to find some meaning and purpose in both. Christianity is no exception. In considering this deepest of all problems in faith I want, as best we can, to go to the gospel record for the answer. As I watch Jesus in his brief years on the stage of history, listen to his teachings, and contemplate the way in which he viewed the twin mysteries of life and death, I find several consistent attitudes from beginning to end. To begin with, Jesus is a realist. He believes in cutting

The Meaning of Sainthood

through the superficial aspects of man's existence to the heart of the problem. As a realist, he does not deny the fact of death. He accepts it, he faces it without flinching, and does what he can to postpone it in his healing ministry.

The thing which matters to Jesus is not the death of the body, but the death of the soul. "And do not fear those who kill the body," he says, "rather fear him who can destroy the soul" (Matthew 10:28). His realism, however, does not separate the two as far as this world is concerned. The enemies of the soul come more often from within the body the soul inhabits; its appetites, its passions, its self-indulgence. Likewise, our bodies suffer from the evil spirits inflicting the soul: bitterness, hatred, self-pity, low aims. These things kill as every physician knows. Soul and body are all of a piece, but in the last analysis, Jesus maintains that whereas the godly must die as all living matter must, the soul need not, if it has managed to achieve certain internal qualities worth preserving. And insofar as a man does that, death has control no more. He is free from the fear of it. He has pulled its sting.

It is precisely this which Jesus himself does when he goes to his death on the cross. His enemies would kill his body, but they never killed his spirit. Even in the agony of his pain, he never stopped loving those wretched men who hung him there. Even when he died, he was confident that his spirit was in God's hands forever. The justification for that triumph is amply proven in that beginning with his sorrowing friends and continues until now. His spirit, his conquest of sin and death, is shared with lesser men like you and me.

It is this which gives significance to the concept of sainthood, expressed in the festival of All Saints. I suppose there is no term about which we have more hangups than the term, saint. It was a sad day for that concept when the church began creating an official role of special people who then had a monopoly on the term. Canonization almost destroyed the meaning of sainthood as found in the New Testament. Halos and stained-glass windows almost finished the job.

To be sure, special people have arisen from the ranks of Christ's followers in every generation. Leadership is a necessity, and our religion cannot survive without leaders. So we do well to remember Mary, Peter, Paul, Augustine, Francis, Martin Luther, Wesley, Phillips Brooks, and countless others who, over the centuries, have been leaders of Christians in their own generations. It is interesting to note that even among the apostles, only Peter and Paul stand out in clear outline. The rest are names, appearing only in the yearly calendar, which would long since have been forgotten were they not recorded as Jesus' intimates in the gospel record. Yet, it is ridiculous to suppose that Peter and Paul did all that was done in the first century to set Christianity on its way as a world religion. A leader is no leader without followers, and the followers as well as the leaders claim whatever praise there may be for what was done for Jesus in their own day.

The Meaning of Sainthood

Not even these great persons of Christian history were flawless. Nor did any claim to be so. Perfection is not, nor has it ever been, the mark of a saint. When the saint has done his best, he still thinks of himself as an unprofitable servant who simply was not always equal to the impossible task laid upon him.

There is also no stereotype of sainthood, no special form of piety which is recognized above all others, no special service to the Lord Jesus which is superior to others. So there are contemplative saints and activist saints, learned and unlearned, aristocrats and common people, those who withdraw from the world and those who act in the world, clergy and lay people. There is no color line drawn in sainthood, no particular nationality or race.

It is all this and more which the church happily recognizes on its festival of All Saints—a cloud of witnesses which encompasses us is such a great multitude that they cannot be counted. They come from all nations, all races, all peoples. They are, if you will, the saints anonymous, those whose names are forgotten as ours will be a few years hence. Their names are known only to God. But they have two things in common. Their imperfections and sins have been taken away, and all the soiling of birth has been washed away in the blood of the lamb whom they served to the best of their ability. And above all else, they share a common loyalty to a master who has taken the simple, fallible, and mortal stuff of humankind and given to it an eternal value.

That value is above all else the victory over death. The might of the Roman Empire could not prevail over the Son of Man and his gospel. Neither could the sin and inadequacy of his followers, nor the disease of their mortal bodies. But that really tells us who these blessed ones are. They are the humble, the sorrowing, those who crave righteousness as they crave food and drink, the merciful, the pure in heart, the peacemakers, the persecuted. These are the ones who have survival value, those whom the death of the body cannot touch. These have the marks of sainthood toward which you and I are called by the Lord Jesus.

So when you say, as we all do on occasion, "of course I'm no saint," think again as to what you mean. If it is mere humility which moves you to say that, well and good. But if you use that expression as an excuse for not doing your best, as an alibi for your failures, God have mercy upon you.

Someone has defined a saint as a sinner who keeps on trying. To God I suspect it is the trying that counts. How hard are you trying?

39

The Uncomfortable Pulpit

A POPULAR book of some years ago was called *The Comfortable Pew*. It was a witty but scathing attack on the Church and church people by an able Canadian of Anglican background. While aimed at lay people, it did not spare the clergy because obviously, if the layman is too comfortable in his pew, the man in the pulpit is not doing his job. There is more than a little truth in the old adage, "like priest like people."

The gift for speaking and the opportunity to use that gift to influence others is about as terrifying and dangerous a gift ever given to man. By it a demagogue like Hitler could transform an able and decent people into a nation of madmen. On the other hand, Winston Churchill could move a beleaguered and hopeless Britain to stand fast against seemingly insurmountable odds and go on to victory. Particularly in the long history of the Judeo-Christian tradition, the preacher in the pulpit, in the fields, or on the street corners has often been more significant than the priest at his altar or the bishop on his throne. But also in that same tradition, some of the worst pages of religious history have been written by false prophets who use their gifts to adulterate the gospel and lead men down paths utterly contrary to the teaching of Christ.

With this in mind, the box perched high above the congregation is an exceedingly uncomfortable place indeed. I never climb into it without deep misgivings. The prayer I offer before I begin to speak is the most sincere I ever utter. And I never climb down again without wondering whether what has been said was really worth saying or has been heard to any good purpose. Like St. Paul, one is caught between that inner compulsion which cries, "woe is me if I preach not the gospel," and the fear that when I have preached to others that I myself should be a castaway. At the altar one feels secure, sustained by the liturgy and the traditions of the past. This security departs when one enters the pulpit.

The discomfort of the pulpit is due, in the first place, to the amazing presumption that a man should dare to speak for God to other men like himself. The modern preacher is not as explicit as the Old Testament prophets; he does not preface his remarks with the phrase, "thus saith the Lord" as they did. Perhaps we lack their assurance and therefore confine our messages to speaking *about* God rather than *for* God. Not that speaking about God is unimportant or has no place in preaching. It is important that believing men know what the scriptures tell us about God, and see for themselves an adequate concept of the one in whom they believe.

Speaking for God is a different matter, and yet without it religion remains rooted in the past, out of touch with the world, with no growing edge and no present awareness of a living moving spirit. As you know, prophets of old were not so much foretellers predicting the future, they were primarily *forth*tellers speaking to their time and place, bringing the God of the past into the present, and catching from him some new insights as to who he is and what his purposes are for mankind. If they mentioned the past or cited the scriptures, it was only to throw light upon the present or to give continuity to the steady unfolding of God's revelation of himself to successive generations and to themselves.

I would remind you also that Paul and the others of the early church did not preach about Christ. There are few references to his specific teachings. Little mention is made of his birth or of the events of his earthly ministry except of his death and resurrection. No doubt the primitive record on which the gospels are based was already in circulation and could be taken for granted. But Paul's concern was solely to speak for the living Christ whom he first met on the road to Damascus and who had been his constant companion and the all-pervading influence on his life thereafter. He was primarily interested in what his Christ could do in the cities of the empire, not in what he had done in the countryside of Palestine. And so our faith broke its bonds to the past by the daring of the men who spoke *for* Christ and not *about* him.

Yet every one of these, from Old Testament prophets to New Testament apostles, was at times terrified by this awesome task. When God appeared to Isaiah at a time of national crisis and challenged him to speak for him at the royal court, Isaiah's instinctive response was to cry out, "Woe is me! I am lost, for I am a man of unclean lips and I dwell among a people of unclean lips" (Isaiah 6:5). So, too, we find Paul wondering at times in his letters why Christ had entrusted to him of all people this awesome task, and quite frankly admitting that he often "spoke as a fool" (2 Corinthians 11:22).

The point is that there is an inevitable identification of the man who purports to speak for God with the men to whom he speaks. Whether accident or not, there is a very deep significance in the placing of the pulpit, not in the sanctuary, but in the congregation, and the man who occupies it has abdicated for the moment his priestly function when he speaks to God for his people, and his preaching function when he speaks for God as a man to men. As a priest he is the conserver of the tradition; as a preacher he is reckless of tradition as he tries to bring God into a dynamic relationship with his listeners.

But in it all he is still a man; he knows what sin is. He often gropes his way through the fog of his times. His mind is finite and cannot grasp infinity. Further, he shares in the virtues and vices of his generation. He is a citizen with a citizen's

The Uncomfortable Pulpit

duties and responsibilities. Part of his work has little direct bearing on spiritual things. He earns money and spends it. He has his prejudices and dislikes. He is not exempt from illness, accident, nor finally from death. He likes the approval of men. He has his virtues and ambitions, his inhibitions and his moods. He is imperfect, inadequate, and utterly incapable of knowing all the truth about God or man, or even of himself. But he cannot possibly speak for a God whom he does not know, nor preach a Christ whose redeeming presence he has not felt. And the test of this is not in what he says, but in what he is as a man among men. Do you wonder then why the pulpit is an uncomfortable place?

It is uncomfortable for yet another reason, and that is the nature of the gospel to be proclaimed. The comfortable gospel is easily misunderstood. There is, of course, comfort in it as we understand that word, comfortable, today. Men have a right to find release from life's tensions and the lifting of its burden. They need forgiveness and encouragement and peace. Men have every right to expect to find all this in church. "Comfort, comfort my people, says your God" (Isaiah 40:1), is an integral part of the prophet's message. And "come to me all whose work is hard, whose load is heavy; and I will give you relief" (Matthew 11:28), is certainly part of the gospel, and if a man is to speak for God I am sure these are things God wants him to say on occasion. But this is not the whole gospel, nor is it what that word, comfortable, originally meant and still should mean.

The word, comfort, is an active term from the Latin *confortare,* and means to strengthen greatly. When Jesus fed the hungry and healed the sick, he was popular and people heard him gladly. But when he began to ask hard things of them such as loving their enemies, they turned away. They liked the comfort, but they didn't care to be strengthened for difficult tasks. When he attacked the institutions of society which preyed upon the poor, the hopeless, and sick, the crowds forsook him. So on both counts he wound up with disillusioned friends and powerful enemies and went to his cross.

After his resurrection he spent forty days comforting his few friends, restoring their confidence in themselves and himself. But when they tried to hold onto him indefinitely, he left them for good so that they could transmute the comfort he had given them into the mighty strength that began on Pentecost, and within a generation, had spread throughout the empire.

Like their master who had been accused of stirring up the people, his friends were accused everywhere of turning the world upside down. They were persecuted, beaten, driven from place to place, and killed, but strengthened by Christ's "spirit in the inner being," as Paul put it (Ephesians 3:16). Our world is turned upside down and I would suggest that it is the Christian's job nowadays to turn it right side up. But this is no easy task. It can't be done by human efforts alone. If it is to be done at all, it must be done by men of fire with

God moving through their efforts for the saving of this lost world. It is the preacher's task not to allow people to sleep in their comfortable pews, but to light a fire which cannot be put out. He must call the shots as they really are. He must arouse, disturb, and convince. He must run the risk of unpopularity and enmity. He must be ready to accept defeat. But if what he has to say is of God, some will hear, some will accept the challenge, and some will choose the hard way of Christ.

Yes, the prophet's voice was stilled many centuries ago. Paul's body is long since returned to the dust in an unknown grave, and the Kingdom of God has not yet come. Men are still lost in sin; strife and bloodshed and violence still exist. But men go on hoping, go on proclaiming the good news, disquieted, troubled, uncomfortable, frightened often. They are driven by an inner compulsion to the most foolish occupation in all the world. The foolishness of preaching.

40

Priesthood

I AM an incurable evangelist. I make no bones about it, nor apologies. Every word that I have spoken from the pulpit, every class I have taught, every personal conference I have had with the troubled and heavy-laden, has had but one purpose—to bring men in contact with the saving power of Jesus Christ. For me, that purpose breathes through the majestic phrases of the liturgy as we offer at God's altar the bread and wine, and receive it back as holy food to our soul's health. For me, that purpose must not be lost in the administration or organization of the financial aspects of parish life. For if it is lost, all other things become meaningless and ineffectual.

Partly I suppose, this passion for souls, this evangelical drive is in my blood. One does not come from a long line of Methodist preachers and expect to obliterate, by his espousal of a different loyalty, that which is part of the warp and woof of his inheritance and upbringing. I love the Episcopal

Church because of the hard travail of soul by which I came into it. It is the church of my own free choice, and I would not have it otherwise. But that can never mean that the imprint of my birth and growth in another communion, where the evangelical passion has reached perhaps its finest flower, can be eradicated.

But this, too, can be overemphasized. We dare not overlook the fact that Methodism itself grew out of Anglicanism, and that the Anglican genius, which is too often called compromise, is in reality a capacity for balancing the various elements which are essential for the ongoing life of the Church. I have found the Episcopal Church a more congenial atmosphere for exercising such a ministry than was that of the communion from which I came. To find in the sacramental life of our church something which, after they are won keeps people in Christ, is a tremendous asset. To have ready at hand a drama of an ordered worship so that faith may be made vivid and real, without being accused of putting on a show, is a great help. The place of confession and the assurance of forgiveness in our public services makes it easier and more natural for people to bring their sins and their burdens to the priest in private, thus adding to his public ministry the wonderful and awesome privilege of the pastor. Yes, the Episcopal Church is a great medium for the winning of souls, if we only did but know it.

There is also, I think, significance in the fact that I began my ministry as a rector of a church named for the writer of the fourth gospel, and have gone in reverse order in the patron saints of the parishes I have served. Luke followed John, and then Mark. It is too bad to leave St. Matthew out, but there was not enough time allotted to me to work under his protection too.

The symbolism in that reverse order of the gospel evangelists lies in this fact: just as Mark is simpler and more straightforward than Luke, and Luke more so than John, so is my approach to this whole business of Christian faith and life. Simpler and more straightforward today than it was fifty-odd years ago. Many things which seemed so important then are not now. The banners carried in partisan causes, the fine distinctions of theology and ritualistic practice, the butting of one's head against stone walls of contrary opinion which made life so complicated then, seem no longer to matter very much. Perhaps this is the inevitable creeping in of aged compromise and conservatism. But I rather think it is the realization, which experience gives, that the fundamental things of faith and life are simple and straightforward, and that we needlessly complicate it all with nonessentials which masquerade as fundamental.

The very nature of these years in which my ministry was cast has made that doubly important, for it has been an age of violence, of revolution, of cataclysmic change in which black and white have blurred into a confused gray. Five months after my ordination, the brittle, false, and greedy world of the roaring twenties collapsed. One month after the beginning of my first rectorate, the Depression, which colored all man's thinking for a decade, began. One year after beginning my second rectorate, the nation was plunged into history's grimmest, toughest, and most inconclusive war, whose prosecution and direct aftermath colored another decade. At about the time I began my ministry at St. Mark's, a decade, which may be known as that of an uneasy peace, began in the battlefields of Korea. Political, social, and economic dislocations, on a scale unknown to past history, have been the constant background of my ministry, and with them the complexities of life have become almost unbearable.

A complex faith will not do for times like these. The bewildered, haunted, fear-ridden soul of modern man needs something simple and straightforward to grasp, just as man similarly needed the same in the Roman Empire of the first century. That ancient world was not saved by the great philosophies of the Greeks, nor by the intricate ceremonial of the pagan religions. Men, then as now, were not philosophers nor theologians, but fallible and frightened human beings, wanting to know what life was all about. And some of them found the answer to that age-old question in the simple story St. Mark had to tell which he had gotten from a rough old fisherman named Peter. It was the story of one named Jesus. A brief story, but one so moving and so simple, that slaves and soldiers and merchants of Rome could understand it, live by it, and if need be, die for the sake of it. Later on, philosophers became interested in that story and tried, as in the gospel of John, to fit it into the best systems of Greek thought in order to make the gospel significant to the learned. But always, from that day till now, the gospel of St. Mark has been a constant reminder that the story itself is neither philosophy nor theology, but a simple statement of an historical fact which the ordinary man and woman can read and understand to his soul's health and to his eternal redemption.

That Jesus of Nazareth came preaching the good news of the Kingdom; that he released men from bondage to sickness and sin; that he lived and talked the life of love amidst the hatred and bitterness of a cruel age; that he trusted very ordinary men and women and, by that trust, made them great; that he died on a Roman cross, the victim of man's hatred, blindness, and stupidity; and that he arose from the grave the victor over sin and death to give us men, until the end of time, the same victory over the same two enemies—this is the gospel Mark preached to another distraught and weary age, this the gospel the children of Mark must preach to this distraught and weary age.

That gospel: simple enough for any and all to grasp, fundamental enough to meet the desperate need of simple men, strong enough to keep us steady and true amidst the storms and stresses of a wicked and perverse generation. I pin my faith on that gospel as I have pinned it through most of this century of chaos and world strife. It does not answer all my questions nor solve all my problems, which is probably a good thing, lest I stop growing or withdraw as Christ never did from the world's confusion. With each passing year, the fundamental questions and the fundamental problems find clearer solutions within my soul. I know I am a sinner, but I also know Christ's saving power. I know how desperately men need him, but I also know how truly he meets that need when we give him a chance. The vain doctrines of modern man, by whatever name they may be called, must ultimately prove their vanity as they break against the rock that is Jesus Christ.

And so I close with some words from an old gospel hymn. "On Christ the solid rock I stand; all other ground is sinking sand."

If not available at your
local bookstore, this book may
be ordered by sending the cover price
plus one dollar for postage and handling
to the address below

Madrona Publishers
Department X, P.O. Box 22667
Seattle, WA 98122